MW00860589

THE BATTLES OF
NEW HOPE CHURCH

THE BATTLES OF
NEW HOPE CHURCH

RUSSELL W. BLOUNT, JR.

PELICAN PUBLISHING COMPANY
GRETNA 2010

The word "Pelican" and the depiction of a pelican are trademarks
of Pelican Publishing Company, Inc., and are registered in the
U.S. Patent and Trademark Office.

Library of Congress Cataloging-in-Publication Data

Blount, Russell W.
  The battles of New Hope Church / Russell W. Blount, Jr.
    p. cm.
  Includes bibliographical references and index.
  ISBN 978-1-58980-748-8 (alk. paper)
  1. New Hope Church, Battle of, Ga., 1864. 2. Paulding County (Ga.)—
History, Military—19th century. I. Title.
  E476.7.B55 2010
  975.8'373—dc22

                                2010006609

Printed in the United States of America
Published by Pelican Publishing Company, Inc.
1000 Burmaster Street, Gretna, Louisiana 70053

For Elaine and Trip

Contents

Preface

In early May of 1864, the Battle of the Wilderness was fought in the thick woodlands of central Virginia and has since stirred the interests and imaginations of students of the Civil War, resulting in many fine histories devoted to that great battle. Not so well advertised and sometimes neglected, another battle in another wilderness more than five hundred miles away was grinding on through the final week of this same month. This one happened in Georgia during the Atlanta Campaign. I believe it deserves its own telling and is the subject of this book.

Historians today generally treat the weeklong ordeal in the Georgia wilderness as three separate battles: New Hope Church, Pickett's Mill, and Dallas, all taking place on an eight- to ten-mile front known as the New Hope-Dallas line. At the time, however, and for years after the war, the soldiers who had fought there usually referred to it only as the Battle of New Hope Church, a polite euphemism for the unholy name they privately muttered among themselves—the Hell Hole. No other name could adequately express their emotions for such a time of perdition where men violently fought under miserable conditions over a snarled, tangled, and inhospitable landscape.

War, it seems, is an erratic animal when choosing its venue. Unlike many of the panoramic Civil War battles where the armies came to grips on rolling hills or open fields, the Hell Hole was hidden in a primitive, junglelike terrain, a place that one war correspondent bitterly referred to as "the midnight corner of Georgia." Like the bloody fight in Virginia's wilderness, the battles and skirmishes that took place in Georgia's Hell Hole were fought in a densely wooded country where soldiers could hardly tell friend from foe. It was a place where two large armies found

9

themselves unable to move, where divisions blundered blindly through a vine-clogged land, and men became disoriented, firing into their own side by mistake. Some would say it was a useless squander of lives since no strategic advantage was gained by either side and, in the end, amounted to nothing more than a speed bump in Sherman's drive to Atlanta.

What then was unique or important about the Hell Hole? There are several matters that should be considered here, which were outcomes of the fight and contributed, in one way or another, to the conduct of the remainder of the Atlanta Campaign. For one thing, there was a change in the philosophy of the timid Southern commander, Joseph Johnston, who began the campaign seeking a chance to attack, but now seems convinced he cannot beat the Federal army from an offensive posture and that his army's only hope for victory is a total defensive strategy. During this same time, Johnston begins to lose confidence in the young warrior John Bell Hood, in whom he had formerly placed great trust. William T. Sherman, on the other hand, learns the importance of keeping his army near its vital supply line, the Western and Atlantic Railroad, while he drives for Atlanta. Finally, and most important, the same conditions that made the fighting so hellish here caused both armies to begin digging ditches and building earthworks and fortifications more formidable than any seen before in military history, thus introducing the awful era of trench warfare.

Some of those trenches are still evident today. Several years ago, I toured the New Hope-Dallas line, purposely timing my visit to happen in late May so I could see how the trees had leafed out at the time the battles were fought. Much of the actual ground has unfortunately been devoured by all manner of development. The original church building at New Hope, near the point where men began killing each other on the afternoon of May 25, 1864, is long since gone. The adjoining cemetery is, however, still there. Also, one of the battlefields, Pickett's Mill, has been acquired and maintained by the state of Georgia. Assuming that site typical of the rest of the land that once comprised the Hell Hole, I began to realize the problems that such a preponderance of troops would encounter when fighting over this ground. The woods are thick, nearly impenetrable, and in a wild primordial state. Even on a guided tour, I felt lost and could only imagine how confused and disoriented men in battle would have felt when these woods were filled with smoke, curses, and flying metal. The narrow trails we followed rambled up ridges then plunged into deep ravines. Along the way, impressions of the sunken earthworks were still visible, and looking through the thicket, I knew that somewhere out there were the mass graves of the fallen soldiers.

Walking the ground may have helped me to imagine what happened, or what may have happened, in the Hell Hole. But to write on any facet of the Civil War, one must rummage through volumes of paper from the past. Since this is a close-up history of one particularly awful moment in a long and awful war, I too have done a good deal of that rummaging. But tedious research alone does not re-create history, nor will it stir the imaginations of its readers. The problem—the everlasting problem—in writing this or any other history was how to breathe life into a pile of old, dusty records without losing objectivity or compromising the integrity of the history.

To try to make this happen, I've strayed from the conventional method of writing history, switching the tense from the standard past to the present. While this literary style is not the norm, neither is it unique. Other writers have employed it—most notably, Albert Castel in *Decision in the West,* a source used often in this book. That style, I believe, is the most effective means of lending some essence of reality to the past. This, of course, is at least an effort to make the reader a bystander or eyewitness to the event. Thus wherever possible, except for introductions, backgrounds, and after-action recollections, I've chosen to remain in the present tense.

Another thing that will be apparent to the reader is a different presentation of the ingredients typically found in battle histories, especially close-ups where a single moment in the war is being narrated. Though not ignored, less emphasis is placed on identifying the various regiments, or following their actions and movements. Neither are command decisions, strategies, and tactics greatly analyzed. Rather I have attempted a historical storytelling, narrated in part through the anecdotes and memorable lines of individual soldiers who endured the Hell Hole. Their letters, diaries, and memoirs give us a sense of the emotional intensities of that ordeal, offering the reader a more insightful appreciation of the battle pieces presented here.

But what of each man's relation to the events voiced in these documents? While they all shared the same hostile experience, the views and feelings of a Union general, say Sherman, were quite different from those of a Confederate private like Sam Watkins. What happens to them in the course of a battle experience—instead of the mere objective recording of facts—will, hopefully, make reading this history have the appeal, power, and enjoyment of a book of fiction.

Acknowledgments

If there's one thing I've learned in writing this, my first book, is that a book doesn't just slip quietly into its covers. Like some unruly animal, it must be prodded, cajoled, urged, and otherwise compelled to go there. Many people have helped in bringing this about, and I would like to express my appreciation to at least some of them.

Because so much has been written about the American Civil War, it's only appropriate that tribute should be paid to those historians who, over the years, have labored so persistently in composing these narratives. Without their scrutiny, analyses, and interpretations, readers would be forced to rely solely on primary accounts, many of which are often indigestible to the untrained eye. Fortunately, the history of the Civil War in the western theatre has been well served by many eminent historians and fine writers who have sifted through mountains of these documents, drawn on earlier writings, and reduced it all into a literary art. Much of what is presented in this book is woven from the earlier works of historians such as Albert Castel, Richard M. McMurry, Thomas L. Connelly, and Stanley F. Horn, to name just a few. To these and many others, I am profoundly grateful.

In addition to these scholars, I am indebted to William R. Scaife of Cartersville, Georgia, not only for the benefit of his knowledge of the Atlanta Campaign, but for his talent as a cartographer and permission to use some of the excellent maps contained in his book *The Campaign for Atlanta*. Another Georgia historian, Dr. Philip L. Secrist should be recognized for providing information on the landscape and other physical features at the time of the battles and for his tireless efforts in the acquisition and preservation of the Pickett's Mill State Historic Site.

Anyone who has spent time researching any phase of the Civil War has spent much of it sifting through the verbal thicket of orders, letters, reports, and other memoranda contained in *War of the Rebellion,* the official government records known simply as the *OR.* Because this book is only a microcosm of that great epic, my research was thankfully limited to a few volumes of the monumental 128-volume paper trail. Nevertheless, like most Civil War histories, the *OR* is my most cited and indispensable source. For allowing me access to this record and providing so much valuable assistance, I thank Cheryl Somathilake and her staff at the History and Genealogy Library in Mobile, Alabama.

For generous help in research into other sources, I am especially indebted to several others. They are Willie R. Johnson, historian with the Kennesaw Mountain National Park; Abie Norderhaug, archivist with the Wisconsin Veterans Museum; Jack Dickinson at Marshall University's Rosanna Blake Confederate Collection; Russ Adams, proprietor of Bienville Books; and James A. Morgan, librarian with the U.S. State Department. To these and many others, who were pestered with my questions, calls, and letters, I extend my thanks.

Before I began writing this book, I felt that I should walk the ground and gain at least some perspective of the "lay of the land" where the fighting took place. To that end, I am much obliged to Chuck Winchester, park ranger at the Pickett's Mill State Historic Site for personally guiding me through the wilderness of that battlefield. I also owe thanks to the staff there and to James Wooten, who gave me an education in weapons and uniforms. While there, I had the fortuitous good luck to find Edwin C. Bearss, renowned scholar and historian, leading the Chicago Civil War Roundtable on a guided tour that I was invited to join and from which I greatly benefited.

For taking a chance on a novice writer and transforming my manuscript into a publishable book, I owe more than I can say to the publisher, Milburn Calhoun, and the talented staff at Pelican Publishing. To be specific, credit should be extended to the editor in chief, Nina Kooij, who, under her gifted eye, oversaw the entire project, and to Heather Green for her excellence in copyediting. I must also express my gratitude to Suzanne Pfefferle for her tireless efforts in promoting the book. To these go my thanks.

To many friends and relatives, I owe a debt of gratitude for lending so much encouragement throughout the writing of this book, especially Roy Blount, Jr., author and Southern humorist, who gave me good advice along with a much-needed charge of confidence. Last, and only because I save the best for last, I thank my wife, Elaine Hartley Blount, not only for her love, support, and encouragement, but also for reading and rereading drafts of manuscripts and providing me with technical assistance—far beyond my grasp—in completing this enterprise.

For everyone involved, whether mentioned or not, I will remain appreciative for their contributions, which hopefully made this a better book. As to any remaining faults and errors, I accept full responsibility.

Russell W. Blount, Jr.
Mobile, Alabama

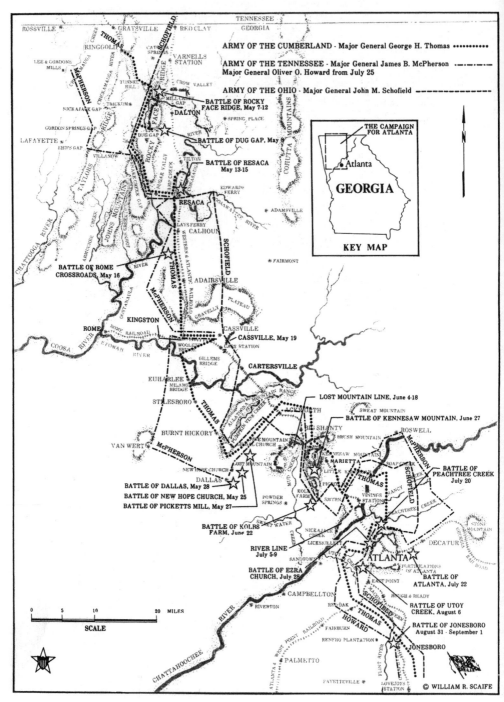

Map of Atlanta Campaign (Courtesy William R. Scaife, Scaife Publications, 1993)

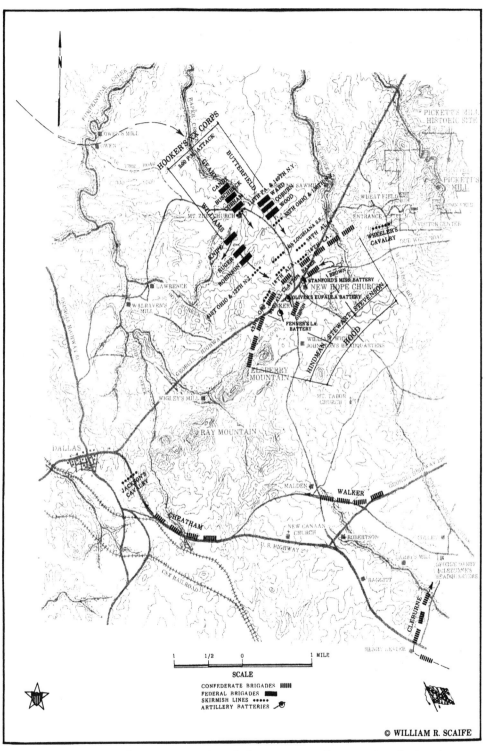

Map of Battle of New Hope Church (Courtesy William R. Scaife, Scaife Publications, 1993)

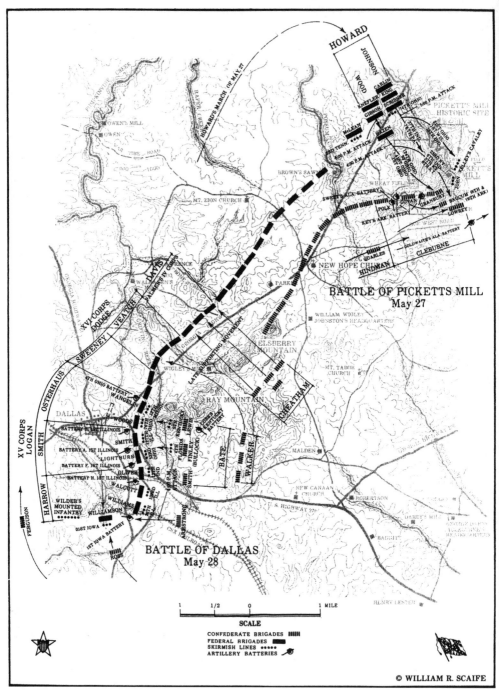

Map of Battles of Pickett's Mill and Dallas (Courtesy William R. Scaife,
Scaife Publications, 1993)

THE BATTLES OF
NEW HOPE CHURCH

Chapter One

Across the Rubicon

A simple hewn log cabin stands on the north slope of Elsberry Mountain. It offers a spectacular view of the dense woods and fields covering the red clay of North Georgia. Standing barefoot on the planked porch, a small boy clutches one of the rough cedar posts, staring down on the panorama. Across the acres of underbrush and trees, he watches as dust clouds begin rising from one of several narrow, serpentine roads that twist and turn around the low hills, dipping through the ravines, and finally converging at a small rustic Methodist church known simply as New Hope.

Since early that Wednesday morning, the boy has seen the long lines of gray-clad soldiers spilling into the churchyard, heard the shouts of commands from officers. Now he gapes at the madness of men rushing about, frantically digging ditches, cutting down trees, and piling them in rows in front of their works. The digging and piling begins in front of the church near the old cemetery then extends north and east till he can no longer see the end of the line of breastworks. Behind the church, drivers curse and crack whips as the wheels of artillery wagons and caissons roar into position. It's a strange cacophony, mixing the clamor of men and equipment with the braying of mules and horses. Still, the clouds of dust continue drifting south toward the tiny church.

****

Shrouded beneath all the stirred up dirt trudges the leading division of "Fighting Joe" Hooker's XX Corps, the center of the powerful Federal army now invading Georgia. The huge army is actually an amalgamation of three different Union armies. Together they total some 100,000 men, five times as large as the population of Atlanta, the state's largest city and their ultimate objective. With them they bring 254 cannons, 5,150 supply wagons, and 860 ambulances, all pulled by nearly 45,000 mules and horses.[1] From Nashville, twenty freight cars a day lumber down the Western and Atlantic Railroad, the artery that has fed the great horde since they left Chattanooga. Like a swarm of locusts, the army has gnawed up everything in its path. It is a machine of war, entrusted to a man who some whisper to be crazy, William Tecumseh Sherman.

At West Point, they called him "Cump," a nickname given him by his brothers and sisters. The soldiers know him as "Uncle Billy." Whatever the sobriquet, Sherman is clearly a man cut from a different cloth. Scarred with wrinkles, he looks older than his forty-four years. He is tall and wiry and has dark red hair and a short matching beard, all surrounding a set of cold steel eyes that stare holes in their targets. He likes to curse, and does it often, especially when it comes to politicians, most of whom he dislikes, and newspaper reporters, all of whom he considers to be pests and spies. He's a kinetic man, pacing floors, never still, and always wreathed in a cloud of smoke drifting from his ever-present cigar.[2]

Sherman is an intellectual sort with a razor-sharp mind. He's cerebral, constantly thinking and agonizing over every decision he makes. Even life's small distractions and aggravations bother him. Whatever the subject, he rarely hides his feelings. Those around him are bombarded with his incessant, rapid-fire speech, emphasized with quick, nervous gestures. With such a temperament and lively personality, he is the extreme opposite of his superior, Ulysses S. Grant, now the supreme commander of the United States forces.[3]

During the course of the war, Sherman has won the confidence and admiration of the quiet and introverted Grant who appreciates Sherman's loyalty and devotion to the Union and has tapped him to command the army in the West. What Sherman needs, and has always needed, is direction and a purpose, which Grant gives him. The plan is for Sherman to drive for Atlanta, crushing the Confederate Army of Tennessee while Grant destroys Lee's army in Virginia. The simultaneous effort, as Grant sees it, will keep the two Rebel armies from reinforcing each other as they had successfully done in the past.[4]

William T. Sherman (Courtesy Prints and Photographs Division, Library of Congress)

To Sherman this is more than an order from above. Grant is his friend, maybe his best. It's a strong friendship, tied together by the misery and glory of war. Earlier in the war both men had weathered the criticism of their character flaws: Grant for his drinking and Sherman for an emotional breakdown he had experienced in 1861. A sort of mutual empathy then developed and helped create a bond between one ridiculed for being a drunk and the other labeled as crazy. Both were, in a sense, outcasts. But at the battle of Shiloh, their friendship was solidified, and both proved they could fight. Aside from the differences in their personalities, the two are similar in some ways. These West Point graduates have experienced their share of disappointments and failures in the past. Neither presents an image of one who would command the largest armies ever assembled on the continent. Sherman, like Grant, sports the rumpled uniform bearing gravy stains with few signs of rank, and both are forever engulfed in billows of blue cigar smoke. Whether he looks the part or not, Sherman, at the behest of his friend, now finds himself in that role and in the middle of one of the more remarkable adventures in the history of the United States, an adventure that won't end until he reaches the coastline of the Confederacy. Moreover, during this experience, he will redefine the meaning of war, showing its ugliness to soldier and civilian alike.

On May 21, 1864, Sherman's army pulls up at Kingston, Georgia, on the north bank of the Etowah River. "The Rubicon of Georgia," he philosophically remarks in a wire to his quartermaster.[5] Since moving his army forward on May 5, he has experienced little difficulty. True, there had been the battle at Resaca the week before, but for the most part everything is right on schedule. He has used his numeric strength to pull one flanking movement after another, and the Confederate Army of Tennessee continues to backpedal. Supplies, too, have been plentiful. To this point, he has enjoyed crossing rich fertile ground covered with farms and plantations that yield forage of wheat, rye, and corn, and his supply trains from Chattanooga continue to clatter unmolested down the tracks of the Western and Atlantic rail line.

Sherman, however, knows the difficulties that await him beyond the muddy river. In 1844, as a young lieutenant of artillery, he had passed through this land. "I had ridden the distance on horseback and had noted well the topography of the country," he remembers.[6]

Gone are the sprawling farms, fields, and plantations, replaced instead with mountains, hills, ravines, and knobby ground, all thick with trees and tangled underbrush. In addition to the rigorous terrain facing the army, his soldiers will find little to confiscate from the inhabitants who are, for the most part, women and children, destitute and living in poverty. "The country here is very desolate," writes an appalled war correspondent, "not a house more attractive than a miserable cabin can be seen. There are no fields nor gardens, nor sign of verdure nor tillage. The population, like the soil is poor and disaffected. Most of the men are off in the woods, and the women are silent, ignorant and surly. It is the midnight corner of Georgia."[7]

More troubling to Sherman, however, is the path that the railroad follows. If he pursues the important supply line across the river, it will take him through the Allatoona Mountains, a narrow gorge some eighty feet deep that offers the perfect geography for his army to be trapped and defeated. The pass, he admits, "would be hard to force," and thus he resolves not even to attempt it.[8] With all of the problems lying before him, Sherman decides to stop in Kingston, for a few days at least, to replenish his supplies, rest his army, and mull over his next move.

In a small frame house near the railroad depot in Kingston, Sherman sets up his headquarters. Here he studies maps and reports, trying to determine some way around the Rebel army that is waiting for him to pass through the jagged mountains at Allatoona. Over the next three days, he paces, billows cigar smoke, and scribbles orders and directives. This is also an opportunity to write letters to his brother, John, and his wife, Ellen. "I have no doubt you will complain of neglect on my part," he writes Ellen, "but you have sense enough to see that my every minute has been taken."[9] Theirs has been a strained and unusual relationship. He had grown up with her as a stepbrother, having been adopted by her father, the Hon. Thomas Ewing, when he was nine years old. Over the years, he had grown to love her, and they were married in 1850. Adding to the woes of his emotional breakdown early in the war, they had lost their son, Willie, to typhoid fever in the fall of 1863. It was a loss that grieved them deeply. "Of all my children," writes Sherman, "he seemed the most precious."[10] This and all the tribulations surrounding the war have caused them to become closer, and Ellen is his confidant.

Writing his brother, John, Sherman confides his plan to leave Kingston and skirt around the formidable Allatoona pass: "I propose to cross the Etowah here, and go to Marietta via Dallas."[11] This, of course, means that Sherman will be forced to temporarily leave the railroad, his vital supply line. The detour, however, should not take long. Dallas is only about fifteen miles south of the Etowah. After reaching that point, he will press back to the east another fifteen miles, rejoining the railroad at the town of Marietta. This, he believes, will force the Rebels to abandon their strong defensive position at Allatoona, causing them to retreat to Marietta or perhaps across the Chattahoochee River with their backs to Atlanta. In any event, he doesn't expect much opposition in this maneuver. It will be another grand flanking movement and a safer course, or so he hopes.[12]

On May 23, 1864, at several crossings, Sherman pontoons his huge army across the Etowah River, weaning it from the railroad and pushing southwest toward Dallas, Georgia. He clicks off a telegram to the quartermaster in Nashville: "We are now all in motion, like a vast hive of bees."[13] The quartermaster, Lt. Col. James Donaldson, doesn't have to be reminded of "Uncle Billy's" meaning here, recalling Sherman's words before the campaign had begun, "And if you don't have my army supplied, and keep it supplied, we'll eat your mules up, sir—eat your mules up."[14] Impatient, abrupt, sometimes plain rude, Sherman knows how to deliver a message with no misunderstandings, and Donaldson will attend to it, pronto. He will continue pumping supplies by rail to Kingston. From that point, however, Sherman must now rely on his wagons to haul his food and supplies, and he has ordered provisions for twenty days to be loaded on them.[15]

Sherman rides across the Etowah on a fine new horse, just arrived by rail with compliments from the tormented quartermaster, James Donaldson. Riding along next to him is Gen. George Thomas, now commanding the Army of the Cumberland, the largest of Sherman's armies and the "column of direction." They cross the river at a point Sherman describes as "the valley of the Eucharlee, a tributary coming into the Etowah from the south." From there, he later remembers, they "gradually crossed over a ridge of mountains, parts of which had once been worked over for gold, and were consequently full of paths and unused wagon-roads or tracks." Of course, none of the roads that carry them south of the river are much better than the old mining roads and movement along them is painfully slow.[16]

The weather, too, is extremely hot. There has been little rain, and the roads are dry and churning with dust from the columns of men, animals, and trains of wagons driven by feuding teamsters who constantly argue for the right of way. Soldiers are ordered off the narrow and bottlenecked roads and forced to march through the woods and thickets where they struggle to cross "lagoons and small streams bordered with treacherous quicksands." Canteens are quickly drained, and men fall from the ranks. That night, young Capt. Charles Wills writes in his diary, "I never saw so many stragglers as today."[17]

By May 24, Sherman's entire force of three Federal armies is now across the river, doggedly pressing in the general direction of the town of Dallas. Generals John Schofield and James McPherson, two smart, young academy men, both products of the famed class of 1853, command the flanks of the vast army. Schofield is moving immediately to the left of George Thomas while McPherson, on the army's right, is wheeling through the village of Van Wert for a westward approach to Dallas. Between the two wings plods Thomas's powerful Army of the Cumberland, always the main muscle in Sherman's movements. They are marching for the same point via Stilesboro and Burnt Hickory, and Sherman rides with them. "I think I have the best army in the country," he had boasted to Ellen in his last letter, adding with confidence, "if I can't take Atlanta and stir up Georgia considerably I am mistaken."[18]

Although Sherman is not mistaken in his expectations, he is becoming frustrated with the progress his army is currently making. The stifling heat, bad roads, and miserable terrain have slowed his columns to a crawl. Adding to these woes, skirmishers from the Rebel cavalry have suddenly begun popping out of the thick woods, ambushing the marchers and then quickly disappearing into the underbrush.

Throughout the day, forty-four-year-old John Geary, who is commanding one of Joe Hooker's divisions and in the van of the entire movement has been listening to the crackle of sporadic gunfire. He sits rigidly in the saddle and no one can miss him. At six feet six inches tall, he's a gigantic man whose prominent feature is a frowning, foot-long, tangled, black beard. By 1864, Geary wears the star of a Union general and carries the scars of nine battle wounds that may explain his ill humor and short temper. In formal military circles, they refer to the likes of Geary as a strict disciplinarian who goes by the book and is a stickler for rules. A former politician, he has been accused of being an opportunist who will pursue political gain through a laudable war record. Here in the North Georgia woods he will find another opportunity. His orders are to press forward through this vine-clogged wilderness until he reaches a small village known as Burnt Hickory, named for its spooky black hickory trees that appear to have been scorched by fire.[19]

Early in the afternoon Federal cavalry that have been guarding Geary's flank capture a Confederate courier wandering lost in the woods and carrying a dispatch to Gen. "Red" Jackson commanding the Rebel cavalrymen who have been harassing the columns of Union infantry. The message says that the entire Confederate army is moving in the direction of Dallas to intercept them.[20] They immediately take the dispatch back to Sherman, who is still riding with Thomas. He reads it then quickly rejects it as nonsense. He's still confident that the real strength of the Confederate army is perched in the hills surrounding Allatoona, ready to send them all to hell if they pass through that gap. Still, there may be some force in front of him in those forbidding woods. The question troubles him. Who could be waiting there? How many? He's not sure but is satisfied that any Rebel resistance would only be minimal. Tomorrow is Wednesday. He'll know more then. Geary and the rest of Hooker's Corps will bivouac at Burnt Hickory and cross the Pumpkinvine Creek in the morning. If they encounter the enemy, it will probably be nothing larger than a brigade located somewhere around Dallas. If so, he'll whip them there, but his gut feeling tells him the enemy is nowhere near.

Chapter Two

Old Joe

As Sherman crosses the Etowah, Joseph E. Johnston, from a house just north of Allatoona, goes about the business of managing the South's second largest army. Except for the Confederate president, Jefferson Davis, most everyone likes the fifty-seven-year-old Johnston. A small-framed man, he's neat and dapper with kind gray eyes and a high forehead made even more prominent by his baldness. "In his dress he was a perfect dandy," observed an admiring Tennessee private. "He ever wore the very finest clothes that could be obtained, carrying out in every point the dress and paraphernalia of the soldier, as adopted by the War Department at Richmond, never omitting anything, even to the trappings of his horse, bridle, and saddle. His hat was decorated with a star and feather, his coat with every star and embellishment, and he wore a bright new sash, big gauntlets, and silver spurs. He was the very picture of a general."[1]

Educated at West Point, Johnston has been a professional soldier all his life. He has battled Seminoles, Mexicans, and Yankees and bears wounds from each. Well read and intelligent, the Virginian is a Southern aristocrat by any standard. He is the seventh son of Mary Wood Johnston, a niece of Patrick Henry, famed hero of the American Revolution. In 1845, Johnston marries Lydia McLane, a member of Maryland's privileged upper class, who he will remain devoted to his entire life. It's a strong relationship, having only a single disappointment. Despite the fatherly image his troops see in him, he and Lydia will remain childless throughout their long marriage.[2]

Commanding the Army of Tennessee is not the job Johnston really wants; at least it's not his first choice. After being wounded in Virginia early in the war, he had lost command of that army to Robert E. Lee, a loss he continues to regret. Although he wanted

Joseph E. Johnston (Courtesy National Archives)

another field command, he had, in fact, turned down the job of leading the western army when the opportunity presented itself in early 1863. He only inherits it now because Jefferson Davis had to replace the unpopular Braxton Bragg and didn't have anyone else qualified or willing to command an army. During James Longstreet's service with the Army of Tennessee, Lee's "Old War Horse" had expressed an interest in the job but nothing came of it, and he returned to the more enamored command of his mentor. Lee, of course, would certainly have been a candidate to fill the job, but he wasn't about to leave his beloved Virginia. And, even if he did, who would take the great general's place? Then there was William J. Hardee, the well-respected military scholar of the South and a corps commander in the Army of Tennessee. He was obviously qualified and familiar with that army but didn't want the responsibility and declined the offer. This leaves Davis with only two choices. He can name Johnston, who is the favorite of the Richmond politicians, or the flamboyant Creole Pierre Gustave Toutant Beauregard. The very name gives Davis pain. He has never gotten along with the cocky Frenchman. Moreover, he has already fired him once from this same command after the battle of Shiloh and to reinstate him now would be admitting to a mistake, which to the haughty Davis is not an option. So it all boils down to Johnston. Davis would almost rather swallow poison, but out of choices, on December 16, 1863, he orders Joe Johnston to assume command of the western army.[3]

Johnston and Davis despise each other, and it's difficult to measure or explain that hate. Maybe they're too much alike. Proud and vain, both men are extremely sensitive. Mary Chesnut, the insightful diarist of the Civil War, knows about the relationship. She is married to a high-ranking aide of the president and travels in the best circles of Southern society. Confiding to her diary, she writes, "The President detests Joe Johnston for all the trouble he has given him, and General Joe returns the compliment with compound interest. His hatred of Jeff Davis amounts to a religion. With him it colors all things."[4]

Davis thinks Johnston is a worm, that he's slow, too cautious, and lacks the passion and spirit necessary for victory. He loathes his arrogance, believing that the Virginian and his patrician wife are blue-blooded snobs and condescending toward all westerners, which of course would include the Mississippian Davis. As president, he feels insulted over Johnston's secretiveness, refusing to share with him his strategy and battle plans. In certain military matters, he considers the general's behavior to be petty and uncooperative. This kind of conduct, as Davis sees it, is unbecoming of a general officer and may prove disastrous for the Confederate cause. On top of this, Davis is unhappy over Johnston's political connections. It galls him that the general has developed a sort of alliance, if not friendship, with Texas senator Louis Wigfall, a pugnacious whiskey-swilling politician, dogged in his condemnation of the president.

Johnston's feelings for Davis are equally intolerant, and

probably had their sour beginnings as early as 1855 when Davis, then secretary of war, had denied a promotion to Johnston back in the old army. Johnston is extremely touchy when it comes to military rank believing that, over the years, he has paid his dues and earned the right to the highest command in the Confederate service. Davis doesn't agree and has ranked Johnston fourth among the first five generals named by the government. For a proud and vain man such as Johnston, this was a low blow and one that will never be forgiven. As the war progresses, there ensues a growing lack of confidence and trust between the two men, and the feud continues to swell. Even their wives, who were formerly friends, are now consumed in the fray, constantly making spiteful and catty comments about one another. Johnston also feels that both Davis and his favorite cabinet member, Judah Benjamin, are impractical and meddlesome in military matters. He's disgusted over the fact that the president blames him for some of the misfortunes of war such as Vicksburg, a loss that he believes was inevitable and beyond his control. In short, Johnston considers Davis a poor leader, disagrees with his political goals and military strategy, and, as a consequence, is becoming skeptical about the South's chances for independence.[5]

Johnston's appointment to command the Army of Tennessee only serves to perpetuate the feud between the two men. Both are dissatisfied. Johnston knows that Davis doesn't like him, doesn't want him, and will probably not support him. Moreover, the malcontented Wigfall has convinced him that the president would like to see him fail.[6] Of course this isn't true. Still, Davis, for his part, worries that he was pressured into a decision he may later regret. Given their anxieties, both men would probably have been content if Braxton Bragg had remained in command of the army. However, both understand that scenario is no longer possible because of the disappointing events of the past.

****

Early in 1863 while Johnston was idling away as theatre commander over the western armies, Davis had ordered him to go

Braxton Bragg (Courtesy Prints and Photographs Division, Library of Congress, LC-USZ62-4888)

and investigate the ever-increasing morale problems of the Army of Tennessee and their waning confidence in Bragg. He found the army in winter quarters at Tullahoma, Tennessee, a cold, muddy spot on the road to Chattanooga. One look at the gaunt and nervous Bragg, and Johnston knew that here was a man who had seen his share of trouble. This was not the fine figure of a soldier that Johnston had remembered from the Mexican War. Here was a lean, jittery fellow with a huge set of eyebrows, a tortured look on his face, and seemingly on the verge of a nervous breakdown.

Since the early summer of 1862 when Bragg was appointed to lead the Army of Tennessee, he had experienced a plethora of misery and bad luck. The war in the west had never gone well. The

War Department in Richmond constantly borrowed his troops, sending them throughout the vast territory the Confederate government was expected to defend. Always a concern was the never-ending shortages of military supplies. He had made some bad tactical decisions in battle, most notably at Perryville and Murfreesboro, and had come under criticism from congressmen, newspapermen, and even his own generals. Added to this, his wife, Elise, had become ill and nearly died. Under all the strain, his own health deteriorated. He was plagued with piercing migraines, chronic diarrhea, and a case of mean, red boils, which often kept him out of the saddle. "I am utterly broken down," he finally admitted. These woes contributed to his already hostile disposition and fueled his endless tirades against those around him. The fact that he was unpopular with his troops and despised by many of his generals troubled him most. They didn't like him, wanted him removed from command, and continually let him know it. In turn, Bragg was suspicious of everything his generals did and spent much precious time blaming them for the army's failures and scheming up ways to rid himself of those who criticized him. Cursed by all of this, Bragg had become a physical and emotional wreck.[7]

"No man needed friends more than Bragg," one of his generals had remarked in sympathy.[8] Although Bragg would have never guessed it, just such a friend appeared before him at Tullahoma in the person of Joe Johnston. After reviewing the troops, meeting with the unhappy generals, and listening to the rages of Bragg, Johnston surprised everyone when he sent a glowing report to Richmond claiming the army was in good shape and heaping praise on Bragg for his leadership qualities. Bragg was amazed and delighted to find himself under this shower of unaccustomed compliments. Davis, too, was pleased that he could, in good conscience, retain his general in whom he had great confidence and had always supported. Johnston, however, was not happy. Bored with his administrative position, he would have preferred Bragg's job. He could have told the truth, given Bragg an unfavorable review, and, as his nominal supervisor, taken command of the army. However, that course of action would not have been in keeping with Johnston's personal code of ethics. He simply refused to promote himself at the expense of a fellow general, especially the hapless Bragg. As a result, gentlemanly Joe Johnston continued to be without a field command. And Bragg, like the biblical Job, kept hanging on, even though his days were numbered.[9]

With the president's help and Johnston's endorsement, Bragg managed to hang on to his command until November of 1863 when, in a poorly planned defense, he was chased from the heights of Missionary Ridge, losing forever the prized city of Chattanooga. That finished him. Submitting his resignation to a relieved Congress, a worn-out and haggard Bragg skulked off to Richmond, where he spent the rest of the war cradled under the protection of Jefferson Davis, serving as his military adviser. The following month Joe Johnston assumed command of the Army of Tennessee.

****

On the morning of December 27, 1863, Joe Johnston reports for duty at Dalton, Georgia. There he finds the remains of the Army of Tennessee shivering away the winter in lean-tos and crude huts fashioned from canvas and logs. They are gaunt, raw-boned men, existing on half-rations and stealing food to stay alive. Many of them are shoeless, without blankets or coats. All are in ragged uniforms, undisciplined, and going through the motions of soldiers and nothing more. Dysentery and scurvy are rampant. Still worse, he finds despondency, crushed and weary spirits, reeling from defeat and haunted by the memory of Bragg. In the back of their minds they fret over Sherman, who they know is close by in Chattanooga, making ready to pounce on them with his huge army.[10]

Throughout the early months of 1864, Johnston works feverishly, trying to rebuild the army. He immediately increases the supply trains coming from Atlanta. Rations improve and clothing and shoes are provided. He meets with the generals, reviews the troops, and explores the extent of their capabilities. He orders drills, inspections, and parades, all of which increase discipline and boost morale. Furloughs are granted. Spirits improve and men are actually seen laughing and joking, temporarily forgetting the miseries and horrors of war. They give the credit for this unfamiliar *élan* to their new commander, "Old Joe." "We soon got proud," remarks a Tennessee private, "the blood of the old Cavaliers tingled in our veins." An Alabama soldier is quick to agree, "I never saw more enthusiasm among our soldiers or more eagerness for battle. General Johnston has infused new life into the army." As the mood of the army improves, religious revivals break out everywhere. Chaplains work overtime receiving long lines of men ready to get right with the Lord, and rivers and streams boil with baptisms. In the words of Pvt. Sam Watkins, "A new era had dawned."[11]

"Boys, this is Old Joe," crows Maj. Gen. Frank Cheatham as he introduces Johnston to his cheering Tennessee division.[12] They had marched to their new general's headquarters to honor him with a serenade by a regimental band. As Cheatham makes the introduction, shouting over the blare of the band and the cheers of the men, he reaches over and pats the balding head of Johnston. This, of course, delights the applauding soldiers who are quickly becoming devoted to their new commander. If the pompous Johnston, who had never really liked being called "Joe," was offended by Cheatham's unmilitary display of affection, he never says so.[13]

Besides, Johnston is troubled over matters more pressing than Cheatham's lack of professional manners. Even though the condition and morale of the army has improved, he worries over the paucity in numbers. The army only contains two corps under William J. Hardee and John Bell Hood, probably not exceeding 40,000 able combatants. The cavalry under Joe Wheeler number less than 5,000.[14] Since his arrival at Dalton, Johnston has railed to the War Department in Richmond for reinforcements. The requests are denied or either ignored. Davis doesn't trust Johnston, is satisfied that he has sufficient numbers, and continually nags him to begin an offensive movement. Johnston won't budge, and finally, Davis gives in, reinforcing him with Leonidas Polk's Army of Mississippi, which will become his third corps. Polk's troops begin arriving on May 11 and continue to trickle in from Alabama and Mississippi until Johnston retreats across the Etowah, bringing his infantry strength to 60,000 more or less. And with the supplement of Polk's artillery, Johnston can claim 187 cannons, the most ever assembled by a Confederate army in the west. Still, Johnston realizes that he faces an army nearly twice the size of his own.[15]

On May 5, 1864, Sherman unleashes his monster army into Georgia, and Johnston, in textbook fashion, begins to parry him. As the campaign unfolds, Davis and the rest of the South anxiously watch. As suspected, the prudent Johnston demonstrates his preference for caution over valor, a choice his critics and admirers have debated down through the years. But whatever Johnston is or is not, most credit him as a master of defense. He sees opportunity in retreat, believing the farther Sherman stretches his supply lines, the more vulnerable he will become. At some point, he believes he will find the right moment, the right geography, to turn and strike the blow that will send the Federal army fleeing back to Chattanooga or points beyond. Along the way, he will attempt to check their every movement. As the crow flies, it's about one hundred miles from Dalton to Atlanta, and Johnston intends for Sherman to pay for every inch of it while waiting for the golden opportunity to turn and decisively punish him. If this strategy makes Davis fume, his outnumbered troops find much wisdom in it. Sam Watkins, for instance, writing after the war, remembers Johnston this way: "He brought all the powers of his army into play; ever on the defensive, 'tis true, yet ever striking the enemy in his most vulnerable part. His face was always to the foe. They could make no movement in which they were not anticipated."[16]

Anticipated or not, the sheer weight of Sherman's army moves Johnston deeper into Georgia. From Dalton to Resaca, across the Oostanaula River, through Adairsville and Cassville to the banks of the Etowah, the Rebel army continues to backpedal. Both Johnston and Sherman try to give battle, but only on their own terms. The result is sixty miles of flanking and counterflanking, followed by the long gray lines of a retreating army. "The wagon train has been passing ever since 12 noon and it is now 5 P.M. and still they come," quartermaster clerk Robert Patrick records in his diary on May 17 while watching the great procession. "Johnston is in full retreat," but then adds with confidence, "The thing is not through with yet and they had better mind how they fool with him for they are getting a long ways from their boats with a good army and a cautious man in front of them."[17]

The next day Johnston begins crossing the Etowah, burning the bridges behind him and falling back to the dusty rail depot of Allatoona. By far, this is the strongest defensive position his army has occupied since leaving Dalton. A railroad gorge surrounded by high hills, the position invites attack. Even though Johnston hopes that will happen, he's realistic enough to know that it won't. No one, especially Sherman, would be foolish enough to attack such a place. What will happen, Johnston believes, is that Sherman will try another flanking movement, and he tells his corps commanders to "be ready to move in any direction at a moment's notice."[18] Until that moment arrives, he will wait and rest his army.

While they wait, a telegram arrives from the president. The message is a curt reply to an earlier wire that Johnston had sent informing the president of his retreat from Resaca. "Your dispatch of 16th received: read with disappointment. I hope the re-enforcements sent will enable you to achieve important results." Johnston senses the president's ire and knows that Davis will be furious when he learns that the army has continued its retreat over the Etowah River without giving battle to Sherman. Taking his time, Johnston waits a day then replies, "I know that my dispatch must of necessity create the feelings you express," and then proceeds to offer what Davis will consider to be a lame excuse, or more likely an outright lie, "I have earnestly sought an opportunity to strike the enemy."[19]

These are dark and depressing days for Johnston as evidenced in his letters to Lydia. On May 21, the same day he responds to the president, he confesses to her that he is "very much disappointed to do so little with so fine an army," something he could never bring himself to admit to Davis. And two days later, he writes, "There was never a time when the comfort of your love was more necessary to me for I have never been so little satisfied with myself."[20] While Johnston's sinking spirits concern her, Lydia finds comfort in the knowledge that all is well with her husband's soul. She has seen to that. In a recent letter to Leonidas Polk, the former Episcopal bishop, long-time friend, and now one of Johnston's corps commanders, she explained to him that her husband needed to be baptized. "It is the dearest wish of my heart that he should be & that you should perform the ceremony," she had told him. During the retreat, somewhere near Cassville, Polk forces the issue, and Johnston, knowing he will need a great deal of divine guidance from the Almighty, willingly agrees. Draped in his robe, the bishop administers the sacrament by candlelight, just as he had done for John Bell Hood a week earlier.[21] Cleansed and sanctified, a solemn Johnston turns his attention back to the sinister and unholy business of waging war against his brethren in blue.

At Johnston's headquarters outside Allatoona, dust-covered horsemen from Wheeler's cavalry continue to ride in with word of the Federal army's movements. By May 23, he has determined that Sherman is moving in a southwestwardly direction intent on flanking him again. "The enemy crossed the Etowah near Stilesborough," he wires Davis and assures him that the army is on the way "to intercept him and oppose his farther progress."[22] At dawn the next morning, Johnston sends the corps of both Hardee and Polk marching hard to cut off the advance of Sherman's army. Hardee's corps, in the lead, anchors at Dallas, some sixteen miles from their starting point at Allatoona with Polk forming on his right. Johnston, now certain that Allatoona will not be attacked, orders Hood to follow, extending the Confederate line to a point just northeast of New Hope Church. The line now stretches out for a distance of eight or nine miles following the same general direction as the many ridges and knobby hills that fall from the Appalachians through North Georgia.

All along this line, men begin breaking out picks, shovels, spades, and axes. Instinctively, they begin digging, piling rocks, logs, brush, and anything that will serve to deflect a bullet. These veterans of the Army of Tennessee are about to stumble on a new and deadly kind of warfare, one that will grind on for many days to come. While they labor, they hear the distant report of gunfire, probably cavalry skirmishing. It's not an enjoyable sound. They know that beyond the trace of shots and somewhere out there, through the thick and tangled woods, Yankee infantry must be approaching.

Chapter Three

The Road to
New Hope Church

When John Geary's division awakens and begins to stir on Wednesday morning, May 25, they see what promises to be another beautiful spring day. By 7:00 A.M., the leading elements have begun marching down the narrow road from Burnt Hickory through a dark, junglelike forest that is rioting in new foliage, thick and green. Except for the rhythmic beat of an army on the move, the only sounds in this tranquil setting are the early morning calls of wild birds. The stillness strikes one of the marchers to scrawl in his diary, "It was then so quiet one could hardly imagine the enemy within 50 miles."[1] Little sunlight filters through the canopy of trees except when they occasionally pass by one of the small fields or clearings adjoining the rough farm cabins whose surroundings have been mowed clean by swine and other livestock. Unlike the battle-scarred lands that he has grown accustomed to, Lt. Alexis Cope appreciates the pristine landscape but adds his ominous prediction that "it was now destined to receive its full share of the blighting curse which must fall alike upon all rebellious soil."[2]

It started so calmly that morning. John Geary and his corps commander, Joe Hooker, are riding together surrounded by their escorts and staffs and in the lead of Geary's veteran division. Approaching Pumpkinvine Creek, they see flames licking skyward and immediately realize that the bridge at Owen's Mill is on fire. A closer look tells them the fire has just been set, and if they hurry, the crossing can be saved with only minimal damage. As some of the soldiers rush forward to extinguish the flames, gunshots begin to pop from a hill beyond the creek. Geary, who has suspected that the Rebel army is somewhere near, interprets the little eruption of musketry as a validation of his feelings, "proving that the enemy were here in our front."[3]

41

Always anxious for a fight, even a little one, Geary summons his infantry forward. Before they can arrive, however, a dignified figure riding a glistening black horse charges past him leading his cavalry escort across the bridge in pursuit of the fleeing Rebel skirmishers. "Fighting Joe," some called him, a nickname Hooker had inherited back in Virginia, before losing his job as commander of the Army of the Potomac. After being defeated at Chancellorsville, President Lincoln, who has great respect for his bravery, had sent Hooker to the western theatre where he now commands the XX Corps under George Thomas, the largest in Sherman's army. He is a tall, handsome, well-barbered man with perfect posture, the beau ideal of a Union general. Vain and ever aware of his image, his uniform is clean and creased, his boots highly buffed, and he loves to sit for portraits. He also likes to brag and seldom turns down a drink. Because of his arrogance and self-serving attitude most of his fellow officers, including Geary, don't like him. Sherman despises him, describing Hooker in a letter to his wife as "envious, imperious, and braggart."[4] But because of his political connections, Sherman is forced to tolerate him. And Hooker is now determined to vindicate his earlier failure, be a main character in this war, and establish his place in history. He sees this campaign as his golden opportunity to do so, and he confidently brags in a letter to a friend "that I shall be regarded as the best soldier in this Army if I am not now, provided we have a few opportunities to establish our relative merits." He goes on to say, "I have never yet seen the time that there was no place for a man willing to fight."[5]

The affair at the bridge turns out to be nothing more than a minor annoyance as Hooker and his escort scatter what Geary calculates to be about twenty-five Rebel cavalrymen. The fire is quickly extinguished, repairs are made to the bridge, and the XX Corps resumes its march with Geary's division still in the lead, followed by the divisions of Alpheus Williams and Dan Butterfield. They don't travel far before coming to a fork in the road. Here Hooker becomes confused as he stares down a second road that doesn't appear on his map. The map clearly shows the main road leading to Dallas while the uncharted road veers off to the east. Through some unknown logic, he decides that both roads must eventually end up in Dallas where Sherman has ordered him to

Joseph Hooker (Courtesy Prints and Photographs Division, Library of Congress, LC-USZ62-111519)

go. If he's right his decision merits some logic. His corps will make better time by using both routes, and thus lessen the constant traffic jams caused by so many men, mules, horses, and wagons. So he orders Williams and Butterfield to continue along the main road, which he will soon learn is the only one that goes to Dallas. Meanwhile, Hooker will go with Geary's division down this newly discovered byway.[6]

The woods grow thicker and darker as Geary's men disappear down the narrow road. They travel less than two miles when out of nowhere come shouts and cracking gunfire along the Yankee skirmish line moving in front of the column. Unlike the incident back at the bridge, this seems to be more than a few marauding cavalrymen who couldn't set a decent fire. This time there are Rebel infantrymen, lots of them, flying out of the woods at the surprised bluecoats. They're in strong skirmish lines and don't appear to have any intentions of leaving. Firefights fill the woods

Hooker's Escort Charging Rebels Near Owen's Mill, *from* Harper's Weekly, *July 2, 1864*

on both sides of the road, and Hooker is convinced he must be facing a Confederate force of at least brigade strength.

At first, Geary's skirmishers recoil in confusion. But these men are veterans who, not long ago, had won an uphill and difficult battle in Tennessee, driving the Confederates from Lookout Mountain. They quickly regain their wits, rally, and begin pushing the Rebels back. Many of the soldiers, both Union and Confederate, find themselves momentarily lost, turned around in the smoky woods, and bewildered by the sounds of guns they can't see. In the bedlam, men are captured on both sides. Rebel prisoners are herded to the rear where they are questioned by Hooker and Geary. From these captives they learn that the resistance in their front is only an Alabama regiment commanded by Col. Bushrod Jones and a small battalion of Louisiana sharpshooters. Furthermore, they say Hood's entire corps is waiting for them where the road converges with several others at a little Methodist meetinghouse known as New Hope Church. This is disturbing news. Hooker knows they haven't gathered there for a prayer meeting.[7]

Geary is also troubled. "My division was isolated, at least five miles from the nearest supporting troops. Close in my front was an overwhelming force," he later recalls.[8] Hooker then instructs Geary to deploy his troops along a nearby ridge and take up a defensive position. At the same time, he sends couriers racing to alert Williams and Butterfield that his position is "precarious" and to rejoin him as soon as possible. By now it's 2:00 P.M., and he can only hope that Hood won't attack him before his two other divisions can travel the five miles that separate them.

As the XX Corps hurries to reunite, a frantic Hooker sends word to his superior, George Thomas, alerting him of this unexpected dilemma. Thomas, however, is not a man given to excitement, and one who's impossible to scare. Big and burly, he's a methodical man who moves with deliberate care. Unlike Sherman, "Old Pap," as some call him, is not driven by demons. He's calm with steady nerves and pays no attention to the chaos and confusion that war brings. Although a Virginian, Thomas has remained loyal to the Union and more than once saved the day for its armies in the west. Because of his decision to side against his native state, his family has ostracized him as a traitor and scoundrel, refusing to speak his name. Sherman, on the other hand, likes and respects

Thomas, finding but one fault in his Southern general. He is "slow beyond excuse," complains Sherman, who, by contrast, is in a perpetual state of motion and constantly trying to move his army forward. "A fresh furrow in a plowed field will stop the whole column and all begin to intrench," writes Sherman in a letter to Grant describing Thomas's crawling movements and defensive nature. Then he adds, "I have again and again tried to impress on Thomas that we must assail and not defend."[9]

There's no doubt that Thomas is a plodder and lacks the celerity to suit the hyperactive Sherman. But Sherman also recognizes that the Virginian is an experienced and skillful tactician who will eventually get the job done. After receiving word from Hooker of the enemy activity in his front, Thomas is becoming concerned. More reports from other subordinates begin trickling in, leading him to believe that these woods may be crawling with Rebels. The picture of suspicion is completed when, out of nowhere, Confederate cavalry suddenly appear and start shooting up the wagon train that house his headquarters. This is enough to arouse the stern-faced Thomas to action. He sends Henry Stone, a captain on his staff, galloping off to bring up Oliver Howard's IV Corps as quickly as possible. After delivering Thomas's message to Howard, Stone is returning when, along the way, he spots Sherman standing by the roadside. The general is in his usual state of impatience, smoking like a chimney, and in a whirlwind conversation with another courier. Stone stops and tells him about Thomas's concerns and relates the message he has just delivered to Howard. Sherman, of course, doesn't believe it, and certainly doesn't want to listen to any lame excuses about why his army isn't moving forward. "I don't see what they are waiting for in front now," he quips, "There haven't been twenty Rebels there today."[10]

****

Sherman is wrong. Indeed, the entire Army of Tennessee is perched in front of him, and Hooker is on a collision course with its right wing. That wing is commanded by thirty-three-year-old

John Bell Hood, or at least what is left of the man his friends call "Sam." War wounds have taken their toll on the giant, ungainly Kentuckian with sleepy blue eyes and a thick tawny beard. At Gettysburg, his left arm was nearly torn off in a cannonade and now hangs at his side as a useless appendage. Then at Chickamauga, a rifle ball busted his right leg, leaving him an amputee with only a stump of a little more than four inches. These wounds, especially the last one, would have killed most men. But not Hood, like Rasputin he's hard to kill. Still, the horrible wounds have left him in constant pain, and he often turns to laudanum and whiskey for relief.

Following the amputation of his leg, Hood had gone to Richmond to recuperate. It was good timing for the wounded soldier. While there he spent endless hours cultivating a good relationship with President Davis, which ultimately won him a promotion to corps commander under Joe Johnston. For Davis, Hood was a breath of fresh air, a combative soul who was aggressive, knew how to fight, and always eager to take the offensive. As the days went by, Hood won the confidence and admiration of the president. He was always quick to agree with Davis's ideas about military operations, stroking his ego with such patronizing remarks as "Mr. President, why don't you come and lead us yourself? I would follow you to the death."[11]

Although Hood was a physical wreck, hobbling on a wooden leg, Davis saw a spirit in the young general, a spirit seemingly absent in Johnston whose pomposity, vagueness of strategy, and lack of initiative had finally gotten on his last nerve. Davis believed Hood's promotion would give the Army of Tennessee some of the confidence and energy it needed. Besides, Davis reasoned, with Hood as a corps commander he could keep an eye on Johnston and, at the same time, keep him informed of his plans and operations that, in the past, the general had refused to share with him. In effect, Hood would be the president's spy. It was hardly ethical, but what Johnston didn't know wouldn't hurt him. Or would it?

Hood's stay in Richmond served not only as a time to advance his military career, but a chance to again take up his courtship with the flirtatious socialite, Sally Buchanan Preston, known simply as "Buck" to her well-bred friends. Early in 1863 he had

John Bell Hood (Courtesy Prints and Photographs Division, Library of Congress)

met her and fallen in love—as many before him had—and, from that moment on, was hopelessly smitten. His infatuation was understandable. Buck was a beauty, educated in Paris, bilingual, fashionable, and the product of one of the South's most influential and wealthy families. In Richmond's prominent society, Hood, a war hero, was a celebrated figure, and he managed to show up at any social event where Buck was present. A romantic in love and war, Hood dreamed of winning her hand. Despite his disfiguring wounds, he was relentless in his attempts to marry her. However, that would prove difficult. While Hood was certainly not considered a commoner, he was no match for a woman of her social and cultural background, and her family objected to any such union.

In fact, Hood is a simple man, not especially intelligent, and had barely squeaked through West Point, leaving behind a trail of demerits and low grades. At times, the Richmond elite found him to be crude and oblivious of manners. Nevertheless, before he left Richmond to join the army in North Georgia, Hood's determination and persistence paid off. She gave him a half-hearted consent to an engagement but insisted it remain a secret. Hood was ecstatic. The secret, however, leaked out. And shortly before his departure, at a dinner party with friends, she was overheard denying any such arrangement. "Absurd—engaged to that man! Never—for what do you take me," she exclaimed. Hood, aware of the remark, still remained hopeful; refusing to accept a broken dream, he boarded a train to report for duty.[12]

✵✵✵✵✵✵✵✵✵✵✵✵✵✵✵

Having left Sally Preston and Jefferson Davis behind in Richmond, John Bell Hood is now determined to impress them on the battlefield. Strapped in his saddle in the dense woods surrounding New Hope Church, the sad-faced Hood looks more like an Old Testament prophet than a soldier. But if anyone likes to fight, it's Hood, and he's satisfied one is coming. He dreams of days past when, as a dashing cavalier, he had gallantly served under his heroes, Lee and Jackson, in the Army of Northern Virginia. Such romantic notions are evident in an inspirational order he now writes and circulates among his men and officers. His message is clear "that in the coming battle their country expects of them victory." He then reminds them of Lee's army and "the triumphs which have crowned their efforts," assuring them that if the Army of Northern Virginia can win "against overwhelming odds," so can we. Who could refuse Hood? The Yankees have torn him from limb to limb, and he still keeps coming, ready to take them all on. If the men have any doubt about his resolve, he concludes with the conviction: "Death is far preferable to defeat."[13]

Late Wednesday morning, Hood becomes aware of Federal troops crossing Pumpkinvine Creek and coming down the road toward New Hope Church. He gives a staff officer orders to detach Col. Bushrod Jones's Fifty-eighth Alabama regiment and Maj. John Austin's battalion of Louisiana sharpshooters from the main body to reconnoiter this unseen foe. It seems, according to Jones's after-action report, Hood does not believe that the leading elements of the whole Yankee army have already arrived in his front. "General Hood wished me to advance along that road and drive the enemy back; that they were only mounted infantry and in small force." [14]

It was a mistake but, because of the thick woods, one that could hardly be anticipated. Jones's regiment, with Austin on his left, moves steadily forward through the underbrush and down both sides of the dirt road. After a mile or so they stumble headlong into Geary's skirmish line where rifle fire cracks out, both sides pouring rounds into one another. Jones, who only has 250 men in his regiment, quickly sees he's outnumbered. Geary's force "was largely disproportionate to my own," and even with the added strength of Austin's small battalion, "I could make but feeble resistance," he remembers. Still, they stubbornly contest the ground but are slowly driven back to the crest of a small hill. It's here that another messenger from Hood arrives with written instructions for Jones, telling him "to press vigorously forward, make the enemy develop their strength, and then to hold the position." For Jones, this is an untimely command because, by now, he is already considering whether a further stay in these woods would be prudent. Nevertheless, he must obey Hood's orders. Outnumbered and outgunned, he can think of but one simple strategy. "I thought the best means of holding it was to meet an attack by a counter attack," and this he does. The Rebels charge, driving Geary's men about fifty yards before they are once again thrown back to the hill from where they had come. From that position, Jones's regiment continues firing at the enemy for another ten or fifteen minutes, by which time the blue line begins overlapping them on both the right and left. Seeing his predicament, Jones finally orders a retreat that turns out to be just in a nick of time. "I believe," he later recalls, "that if I had resisted a few minutes longer my entire regiment would have been captured."[15]

Streaming back down the road, the fleeing Rebels reach Hood's lines and stagger wearily through them to the safety of the rear where they will now remain in reserve. Their losses in killed, wounded, and captured, according to Jones, are "very heavy." The official count comes to sixty-one, an alarming number for a small regiment engaged in a skirmish. After his unpleasant experience, Jones reports what he has seen to his division commander, Gen. Alexander P. Stewart, whose troops presently compose that part of Hood's corps fortifying the ground in front of New Hope Church.[16]

The forty-two-year-old Stewart is now aware that his division is directly in the path of the oncoming Yankee army and will be the one to defend against an attack, should it come. A. P. Stewart is the picture of an eminent, no-nonsense college professor— perhaps because he is one. Even though he was educated in the science of war at West Point, he had felt a much deeper calling to be a teacher of mathematics. He's not a secessionist, but when his home state, Tennessee, joined the Confederacy, he left the classroom and followed her into war. He has been with the Army of Tennessee from the beginning and has earned a reputation for competence and "quiet courage" among his men. They don't see, nor can they imagine, the peacetime Stewart standing behind a lectern and scribbling algebraic formulas on a blackboard. Instead, they see a soldier in gray of Scottish ancestry with narrow eyes, fine light-colored hair, and a clever mind designed to solve military problems. Maybe because of his pious nature (he's very religious), or maybe because of his boardlike posture, they call him "Old Straight."[17]

A. P. Stewart, from The Photographic History of the Civil War, *1911,* 10:249

Sitting upright in his saddle, Stewart reacts to the problem before him and begins aligning his brigades in battle order. From left to right, he deploys the Georgia brigade of Marcellus Stovall, followed by two brigades of Alabamians under Henry Clayton and Alpheus Baker. Everyone quickly begins digging shallow ditches then piling brush and logs in front of the thrown-up dirt. Everyone, that is, except Stovall's Georgians, who find themselves standing in the church cemetery where their part of the line happens to fall. Rather than shovel through the graves, they take advantage of the cover afforded them by the many slabs of stone markers dotting the graveyard. Behind them, Stewart places Randall Gibson's Louisiana brigade in reserve. Then, along a line north of and nearly even with Gibson, Stewart's artillery under John Eldridge unlimbers its three batteries of sixteen guns.[18]

There are now some 4,000 troops strung out in front of the tiny church to meet the Federal attack. Joe Johnston, who has ridden to Hood's headquarters, begins to worry about the troop arrangement. Specifically, he's concerned about Carter Stevenson's division, which is located slightly behind and to the east of Stewart's line. They are presently the extreme right flank of his army, and should Stewart's line collapse under the weight of an entire Federal corps, Stevenson's division would be cut off and destroyed. To prevent this from happening, he orders two brigades under Edmund Pettus and John Brown from Stevenson's division to align on Baker's right, thus extending the line in a northeastwardly direction. Johnston then gallops off to find Stewart. Reaching Stewart's lines, he finds the men resting, worn out from dragging logs and digging ditches. Bromfield Ridley, a young lieutenant on Stewart's staff, recalls that moment: "He told us that the enemy were 'out there' just three or four hundred yards, to 'throw out skirmishers and put the division in line' and to tell General Stewart that if the line should break we would lose Stevenson's division back of us on the road."[19] At this late hour, Johnston is probably satisfied he can do no more and rides off, bracing for the attack that is sure to come.

Chapter Four

Every Deadly Missile Rained around Us

Around four o'clock in the afternoon, as great black clouds are gathering in the distance, Hooker has finally retrieved the rest of the XX Corps. This delay has concerned Sherman, who had wanted him to push right in with only Geary's division before the Confederates had time to strengthen their line. However, if Hooker is facing Hood's entire corps, as he's been told by prisoners that may have been proven to be rash, and "Fighting Joe," for whatever faults he may have, is not a rash man. But now he's ready and hurries his corps into battle position. It's a huge concentration of men, numbering about 16,000, mostly veterans of the Army of the Potomac. At Sherman's direction, he places his three divisions on single brigade fronts: Butterfield on the left, and Williams on the right, trailed by Geary, whose division will be in reserve since they have been skirmishing all afternoon. The Union brass believes this formation will have the effect of a battering ram, overwhelming anything in its path. Not only that, but by grouping them tightly, the lines will be more manageable in these tangled woods.[1]

Another hour passes before Hooker gives the order putting the corps in motion. There's a flourish of activity. Bugles blow, flags unfurl, drums roll, and row after row of blue-clad Yanks step off the line. The division of Alpheus Williams moves out first, and in spite of the wild underbrush, thick trees, and rolling terrain, they manage to maintain an almost paradelike appearance. Williams, considered to be one of the Union's best combat officers, beams in admiration at what he describes as "beautiful order," as he rides beside Hooker following the leading line. The fifty-three-year-old, Yale-educated lawyer pushes his division forward through several hundred yards of the gnarled landscape, scattering the woodland animals and screeching birds. Confederate skirmishers are also flushed from their cover and begin bolting pell-mell back toward the cover of their line of works. Seeing this, Williams picks up the pace, ordering his men ahead at the "double quick." They break into a slow trot, losing the semblance of a formation, and start down a wide ravine. "Soon we got within range of the enemy's artillery," he later reports, "and they poured into us canister and shrapnel from all directions except the rear." As the tumultuous roar comes booming down from the low ridge in front of them, it's followed by the repulsive sounds of thuds and punches, as shot and ball meet flesh and bone.[2]

As torrents of fire and smoke pour from the red ditches in front of them, it seems that Williams has hit the business end of a hornet's nest. "The noise was deafening," Sgt. Rice Bull records in his diary that day. "The air was filled with the fumes of burning powder . . . the shot and shell from the enemy batteries tearing through the trees caused every head to duck as they passed over us." Even through the battle racket, Bull can hear "the shouts of our men and the yells of the enemy." A split second later, he sees Archibald McDougall, the commander of his New York regiment, drop to the ground with a mortal wound. "After a discharge from their battery I heard a cry just back of me; turning, I saw the Colonel stagger and fall."[3]

In fact, men are falling everywhere, their skulls cracked, bodies torn, and arms and legs mangled. Desperate for cover, many dive behind trees and logs and begin returning the fire. Col. Nirom Crane notes that although "the trees gave some protection to the men," it was, nevertheless, "a severe ordeal," and "I ordered the men to lie down in order to shelter them as much as possible." Not everyone, however, is able to hug the earth. Williams, for example, is high in the saddle, wheeling his horse through branch and bramble. Although he manages to escape the burning projectiles, his horse is hit. "I heard the 'sug' and the horse made a tremendous leap," he writes, recounting the moment in a letter to his daughter.[4]

After groveling for cover, Williams's division wastes no time in sending thousands of rounds whirring right back into the Rebel breastworks. The firing is so heavy and rapid that his brigades, one after another, begin to run out of cartridges, "until my whole division had nearly expended its ammunition," he writes later. As in most battles, the soldiers have been issued their usual supply of sixty rounds per man, not nearly enough, however, for the unusual situation they now face. One regimental colonel, seeing that his "ammunition was entirely exhausted," improvises in desperation, ordering his men "to collect cartridges from the dead and wounded."[5]

Dan Butterfield's division soon begins pitching into the ravine in relief and support of Williams's stacked-up columns. By this time, musketry and cannonading are reaching the boiling point. When Col. John Coburn, commanding one of Butterfield's Indiana regiments, throws his 550 Hoosiers into the fray, they run headlong into the same storm of fire that Williams's troops have been enduring for nearly an hour. In his after-action report, Coburn remembers the devastating fire they faced while advancing through the ravine: "The enemy poured in upon us a tremendous fire of artillery. Shells, grape-shot, canister, railroad spikes, and every deadly missile rained around us."[6]

Despite the maelstrom of flying metal, few of the men turn and run. Should this happen by chance, their officers are, of course, obliged to shoot them. So those inclined to bolt for the rear when they can no longer bear the strain of battle look for legitimate ways to escape, such as posing as a courier, carrying off the wounded, or feigning wounds of their own. Some even resort to more desperate measures that might take them off the line for good and send them home. Pvt. Martin Jones, for example, one of Butterfield's Michigan men, shoots himself in the foot and is granted permission to go to the rear. However, most of the cowards, or "skulkers" as the troops call them, look for a less sanguinary way to exit the battle. "Hello, Jim, what's the hurry?" Pvt. Uriah Farr, Seventieth Indiana, calls to one of his friends as he races past him on his way to the rear. His friend stops long enough to explain that he had fallen and hurt his leg and was hurrying to the rear for treatment. Farr can't help but notice that "he was making good time for a cripple," then adds the resentful wisecrack, "Perhaps the wind from the enemy's shells and solid shots . . . was helping to force him along."[7]

*Williams's division attacking confederate works at New Hope Church,
from* Harper's Weekly, *July 2, 1864*

✳✳✳✳✳✳✳✳✳✳✳✳✳✳✳

Up on the ridge, kneeling in their shallow red ditches, butternut-clad Confederates are fighting like demons. Sweating, cursing, and spitting tobacco in every direction, the men are frantically loading and firing as fast as humanly possible. Cartridge boxes are quickly emptied, and officers, shouting words of encouragement, order more rounds brought up to the smoky ditches then hand them out to the toiling riflemen. By now, musket barrels have turned as hot as branding irons, burning the soldiers' flesh as they reload. The Federal attack soon spreads out across Stewart's entire front, but some of the gray brigades are hit harder than others. Alpheus Baker admits that while his brigade suffered losses in the attack, "the brunt . . . was borne by Clayton's, Gibson's, and Stovall's brigades." As for Clayton, the brigade commander could not have been more pleased, later bragging, "Men could not have fought better or exhibited more cool and resolute courage. Not a man except the wounded left his position."[8]

Along the Confederate battle line, Stewart can be seen sitting tall on his big roan and calmly urging his men to hold their position. He's an easy target for the charging Yankees, and the men tell him so. As always, Old Straight ignores the warnings and continues riding through the eye of the storm. Passing his son, Caruthers, who is just short of his eighteenth birthday and serving on his staff, Stewart hears the boy call out over the din, "Now, Father, you know you promised Mother that you would not expose yourself today." That admonishment brings howls of laughter from every soldier who is within earshot. *Now, Father,* they hoot, and then jam another cartridge home and keep blasting away. It's obvious they love Old Straight and are willing to hold these ditches or pass on to heaven from them. So when a courier from Joe Johnston arrives asking the general if he needs reinforcements, Stewart curtly replies, "My own troops will hold the position."[9]

Stewart's answer is prophetic, but Johnston, a wary man by nature, doesn't fully enjoy the general's confidence that he alone can hold the line against the numerically superior Federals. Although he appreciates Stewart's resolve in the matter, Johnston, nevertheless, decides to bolster Hood's entire right wing and throw in some troops from Bishop Polk's corps. After marching and countermarching, and all the confusion that ensues when armies move men, some of Polk's regiments finally begin falling in behind Stewart's lines where the heaviest sounds of battle have led them. As men from the Twenty-seventh Alabama regiment sprint forward, they give the Rebel Yell, letting the defenders know that help is on the way. Among them is a twenty-one-year-old private named J. P. Cannon, who after the war will go on to medical school, become a doctor, and dedicate himself to comforting the sick and saving lives. But today, like thousands of others, he is a killer, caught up in the miserable business of inflicting pain and taking lives. In his diary, he records the experience:

> The roar of musketry and boom of artillery mingled together told plainly that blood was being spilled freely and with a yell we pressed on to let Hood's men know that help was near and encourage them to stand to their post. Before we reached the battlefield stray bullets began to strike in our ranks and several were killed and wounded. Just in rear of Hood's line, we were halted and found that both sides were merely holding their own. We rested a few minutes, and somewhat recovered our breath, when we were ordered forward. Then came the "tug of war." The Yanks contested the ground stubbornly, and the carnage was fearful.[10]

As the soldiers of Alabama regiment make their way toward the front line, they pass through Eldridge's artillery. His cannons are in full bloom, bucking and roaring. The noise is incredible. It's a jumbled mass of indiscernible racket, completely drowning out the single reports of rifles. Then, as if God has decided to join in the raucousness, thunder and lightning begin to roll and crack from above. "In the midst of the din there was one mighty peal of thunder," remembers an Ohio lieutenant, "so loud, so deep, so profound that we were awe-stricken. It made our heavy guns sound like the snapping of matches in comparison." For the soldiers, it seems as if the forces of heaven and earth are crashing and clapping together in a wild and violent fury. The roar is so deafening that blood begins streaming from the ears of one Confederate artilleryman.[11]

As far as Atlanta, some twenty-five miles away, worried citizens can hear the distant rumbles of battle. If those ominous sounds cause anxiety in Atlanta, as one of the newspapers reports, surely they are creating panic in Marietta, a town much closer to the fighting. Only two days before, while the guns were still roaring beyond the Etowah and rumors of Sherman's approach were flying, Robert Patrick noted in his diary, "The whole town was in an uproar and confusion." Patrick, still with the retreating supply trains, watched in dismay as "citizens of all ages and sexes were hurrying to and fro; Negroes were staggering along under a weight of heavy trunks and boxes; wagons were standing at the doors of private dwellings, being hastily filled with the personal belongings of the owner." Those who weren't busy packing their possessions were "standing about in little groups as if undecided what to do." But today, with the noise of war so close and threatening, many more will join the long lines of refugees streaming south to Atlanta, or points beyond.[12]

Only a few miles away, on the wooded battlefield, the ground is shaking under the men of John Eldridge's artillery battalion. Sixteen guns of various gauges, although somewhat exposed to Yankee rifle fire, have been well placed, and in Hood's words, "Did great execution in the enemy's ranks, and added much to their discomfiture." Across the way, on the Federal side, John Geary, who is certainly no stranger to the experience of a cannonade, agrees with the Rebel general's assessment as to the effect of their guns; and he later admits, "The discharges of canister and shell from the enemy were heavier than in any other battle of the campaign in which my command were engaged." Hood's chief of artillery, Col. Robert Beckham, summoned to take personal command of the slaughtering guns, is now supervising the deadly discharges. Hooker, on the other hand, doesn't yet have the benefit of his artillery, which is still being brought up. And so it seems that the belching Rebel cannons are making all the difference in this fight. Repeatedly, the bluecoats rise up from the protection of their cover and start up the slope, only to be mowed down by the ravaging guns. From the Confederate lines, Lieutenant Ridley watches the destruction in awe. "Like surging waves against the beach," he writes in his journal, "line after line vanished." Before the day is over, nearly 1,600 rounds from the Rebel cannons will be blasted into the faces of the men who make up these vanishing lines.[13]

The business of getting off this many rounds against the Federal infantrymen swarming toward them through thick woods is no easy task. It's dangerous and backbreaking work, and the gun crews are sometimes exposed to enemy fire. To load and fire one of these pieces is a complex routine requiring the concerted effort of four to six men. Besides being the targets of choice for Yankee riflemen, the artillerists face other dangers as well. Muzzles cast from faulty iron occasionally explode, killing or maiming the crew. Other times, in the fracas of battle, half-ton horses or stubborn mules that pull the caissons go berserk, spinning and rearing, crushing or stomping soldiers to death. Such accidents are typical, and at least one is recorded at New Hope Church when Lumsden's Alabama Battery is being moved forward to the firing line. Somewhere in the madness, a gunner trips and falls and is rolled over and crushed beneath the wheel of one of the huge guns.[14]

As the sky grows black and a storm threatens, troops from Thomas Ruger's brigade of Williams's division have somehow managed to work their way through the smoky underbrush to within fifty yards of a Rebel battery they intend to silence. Consequently, Capt. Charles Fenner's Louisiana battery suddenly finds itself nearly blasted out of existence in a barrage of bullets from Ruger's men. Three brothers named Brigdens and a corporal, W. H. Brunet, are manning one of Fenner's guns. The oldest of the Brigdens, who is working as rammer, is quickly killed along with the gunner, Corporal Brunet. Another of the Brigdens grabs the staff, taking over for his dead brother. He too is shot down with a severe wound. The third and youngest brother then steps up in the place of his fallen siblings and miraculously survives the attack. Later, he witnesses the carnage. Sprawled among the big guns, in the sulfurous haze, forty-three men and forty-four horses are dead or wounded, his brothers lying among them.[15]

✳✳✳✳✳✳✳✳✳✳✳✳✳✳✳✳

At 7:00 P.M., with the battle still raging, the growling thunderclouds finally ripen and erupt into rain. It comes in drenching, cold sheets, falling hard and blowing sideways across the darkened sky. "It was a furious storm," Union sergeant Rice Bull records in his diary. "The rain came down in torrents, the lightning was blinding; then the darkness so black it could almost be felt." Between the bolts of lightning, the soldiers can see only by the flashes of light supplied by the muskets and artillery. The fight continues through the storm, and Bull recalls, "For a time the thunder drowned out the sound of the artillery which continued to pound away at our line."[16]

Behind the Confederate lines, Pvt. Hiram Smith Williams, a member of Hood's Pioneer Corps, idly scribbles in his diary as the battle roars away in the distance. To Williams, it is "the heaviest fire I ever listened to." His company has just finished building the hospital arbors under which the surgeons will treat the wounded and perform their grisly amputations. Now he watches as the brigade ambulances begin to roll in from the front, one after another, all "loaded with wounded. You can see all kinds of wounds, slight [and] mortal." Williams, more than most, hates the war and sees this day as another one of "wholesale murder," wishing it would finally end.[17]

And so it does. Somewhere between the raging storm, the darkness, the lack of ammunition, and the mounting casualties, it dies as suddenly as it started. The cannons grumble to a halt, and the musketry dwindles to a sputter. Hooker's troops, like a disgruntled crowd, begrudgingly turn and begin a quiet and sullen withdrawal. There is a short lull before the sounds of wild cheers echo from Stewart's ditches, filling the night.

Chapter Five

The Very Woods Seemed to Moan and Groan

Flashes of lightning illuminate Hooker's men as they grope through the rainy forest back to the ridge where they had started their advance. With shouting staff officers forcing their way through the tangled troops trying to restore order and reform the broken regiments, the scene is confusing. Adding to the chaos, Oliver Howard's IV Corps is now pushing forward in relief of Hooker's men who are falling back, resulting in a situation that Capt. John Tuttle describes as being "without the slightest regard to organization for that was impossible." According to Tuttle, who has become separated from his unit in the turmoil, "Thousands were crowding forward to relieve those who had been fighting," and they have run headlong into thousands of Hooker's men, who "came back in swarms, some carrying or leading their wounded comrades. . . . All was hurry and confusion and nearly everybody was swearing at the top of his voice." The night is pitch-black, and along the roadside, there are large numbers of stragglers who have built fires. But even with the fires, "the darkness [is] almost impenetrable," remarks an Ohio officer. Tuttle is quick to agree, "It was so dark one could not see his hand before him."[1]

The rolls are called again and again, but many don't answer. They are among the dead and wounded still lying on the wooded battle line. Through the rain and darkness come the cries of shot-up soldiers relentlessly begging for help. "It was truly heart rending to hear the groans of the wounded along for miles," laments Captain Tuttle, who continues searching through the dark for his regiment. Torches and lanterns are lit, and corpsmen and stretcher-bearers are sent stumbling through the black thickets gathering the bodies they can see. Those found are taken to the field hospitals where the surgeons are dealing with the bloody aftermath. Oliver Howard, having just arrived with his corps, enters one of the hospitals and witnesses the day's carnage. "On that terrible night the nearest house to the field was filled with the wounded," he remembers. "Torch-lights and candles lighted up dimly the incoming stretchers and the surgeons' tables and instruments. The very woods seemed to moan and groan with the voices of the sufferers not yet brought in."[2]

From what little he's able to see in that dim light, Howard surmises that this has not been a good day for Sherman's army. Earlier in the afternoon, George Thomas had ordered him up in support of Hooker, and he hadn't arrived in time to join the battle. Now surveying the horrible sights around New Hope Church, he worries that he will become the object of criticism and blamed for Hooker's failed assault. Rejecting any such censure directed at him, he makes it clear that the fault wasn't his. "I did so move forward as promptly as possible the moment I received word I was needed." As to his tardiness, he later explains, "My command came up over roads deep with mud and obstructed with wagons." When he finally reached the front, he met Hooker, who had already sent a staff officer telling Howard that he was "hard pressed." Howard then ordered his lead division under John Newton to fall in on Hooker's right. "By the time this was effected it was completely dark," he later claimed. As for his other divisions, it was "too late to locate them otherwise in the thick woods," where they had gone to bed down for the night.[3]

Whatever excuses Howard may offer for his part in the misfortunes of the day won't really matter to Hooker, who has small use for his counterpart anyway. After all, this wouldn't be the first time Howard has ruined the day for Fighting Joe, who still blames him for the defeat at Chancellorsville and ultimately his loss of command of the Army of the Potomac. Hooker can't forget that it was Howard's flank that had collapsed on that day under the weight of Stonewall Jackson's vicious charge. So his tardiness today only adds to Hooker's low estimate of a general who some consider to be even slower than George Thomas, who had been cracking the whip over Howard all afternoon to hurry his corps along. But Howard doesn't have to worry about Hooker's opinion, or for that matter anyone else's, because Sherman, who has the only opinion that really counts, likes him. Although the

Oliver Howard (Courtesy Prints and Photographs Division, Library of Congress)

thirty-three-year-old former instructor at West Point has a history of poor military decisions and tactical errors, Sherman sees his qualities and appreciates Howard, describing him in a letter to Ellen as "a man of mind and intellect" and praising him as "very honest, sincere & moral even to piety but brave having lost an arm already." That arm was lost when Howard was fighting on a battlefield in Virginia, and his empty sleeve reminds everyone of his bravery. What's more, Sherman values his loyalty and devotion to the Union as a lifelong soldier.[4]

Apparently, Oliver Howard, called "Old Prayer Book" by his troops, is not present when several of the generals assemble around a campfire to discuss the battle. As an evangelical tee-totaler, he typically avoids gatherings where there will be drinking and cursing. And since Hooker is present there will probably be no shortage of either. Standing around the fire in a drizzling rain, Alpheus Williams is the center of attention and relates the little meeting in a home letter: "Everyone congratulated me on the splendid manner my division made the advance. Gen. Hooker said to me 'It was the most magnificent sight of the war'; that in all his experience he has never seen anything so splendid." Even though the attack had failed, Hooker is so impressed with the gallant charge of Williams's division that he tells Williams he plans to have Dory Davis, the artist for *Harper's Weekly*, memorialize it with a sketch. And this he does.[5]

Although Williams receives Hooker's praises, no such accolades will be coming to Hooker from the frustrated Sherman. Conversely, Sherman is unhappy with Hooker for delaying the attack to wait for Williams and Butterfield to arrive and holds him responsible for the defeat. As Sherman sees it, the delay had given the Confederates time to reinforce. This reprimand throws Hooker into a rage. From the rumored accounts of some Union soldiers present, Hooker's insolent reply was that fifty more Rebels may have reinforced the enemy's position, and what difference could they have made? For Hooker this is just another instance of Sherman's indignity toward him, prompting him to remark in a future letter to Williams, "I know that he is crazy." While Sherman's insult that evening distresses Hooker, he isn't especially sunny over the casualty list handed him. If the butcher's bill is correct, his losses total 1,665 killed, wounded, or missing. Of these, 302 are listed as missing, and Hooker regrettably admits, "The dead lying between our line and the enemy breastworks we have not been able to recover. This will increase the number of killed and decrease the missing."[6]

At 9:00 P.M., after his unpleasant altercation with Hooker, Sherman sends a note to McPherson, the commander of the army's right wing near Dallas. He tells his general about Hooker's afternoon fight and gives him orders for tomorrow. It seems that Sherman is still not convinced he is facing the entire Army of the Tennessee but does admit that at least one corps is in front of him and maybe more. "We are in dense woods, and see but little, but infer the enemy is behind hastily constructed log barriers," he tells McPherson. "I don't believe there is anything more than Hood's corps, but still Johnston may have his whole army, and we should act on that hypothesis." But whoever is in his front, he plans to attack them at first light, assuming "the enemy has not disappeared in the night." Obviously, Sherman believes there's a good possibility they will be gone by morning. After all, he's not sure to what extent he has damaged Hood. After seeing the chaotic condition of his own troops, he infers, "I am sure similar conditions existed in the army opposed to us, for we were all mixed up." Tired, wet, and frustrated, Sherman then decides to get some rest. "I slept on the ground, without cover, alongside a log, got little sleep [and] resolved at daylight to renew the battle," he later remembers.[7]

The rain, occasionally heavy, continues off and on throughout the night while the dead and wounded are still being recovered and brought to the field hospitals. No one sleeps much. Who could sleep on such a night filled with the pathetic whimpers and cries of the wounded, not to mention the aggravating downpours of rain? Besides, there is work to be done, important work that may save lives. "About ten that night we began to build rifle pits," Sergeant Bull records in his diary. "We had to work quietly as the enemy would send a shower of bullets after any unusual sound."[8] Up and down Hooker's lines lanterns, like fire flies in the night, bob and weave over the ditches and pits where the men are working. They dig with picks, shovels, bayonets, tin plates, or anything that will serve as a tool to grub out a hole in the wet, red dirt. Others, armed with axes, hammer and slash away at trees and logs, and then drag them through the bramble to their breastworks. Just as Sergeant Bull has pointed out, the work will stop from time to time, and men will scurry for cover when Rebel snipers fire blindly into the night. However, their only targets are sounds from the work, or the flashes of light from lanterns and torches. The interruptions are brief, causing no real danger, and the work soon continues.

****

Hooker's men aren't the only ones fretting over the protection of breastworks. Southerners, expecting another attack in the morning, also labor through the night improving and extending the primitive fortifications they had started earlier in the day. "We are getting to be expert with pick and spade," brags Pvt. J. P. Cannon who, like most others, never complains about digging the

The artillery-torn forest near New Hope Church (Photograph by George N. Barnard)

ditches that "protect us from the bullets and fragments of shells which are continually flying around and about us." Both sides, it seems, experience the same difficulties while digging for their safety, as is evident when Pvt. Hiram Williams complains, "The firing between the pickets was kept up all night long, so as to keep the men on either side from working on their breastworks. . . . My Regiment, however, managed to get very fair works erected." Williams, like everyone, will appreciate the importance of these works as the hours and days pass. Even now, it's obvious that the hastily dug, shallow ditches the Confederates had fought from on this day had made a significant difference in the loss of lives. Stewart, in fact, reports casualties in his division as being somewhere between three hundred and four hundred men, a fraction of what Hooker has lost in the very same time.[9]

But figures don't bleed and suffer, and they certainly don't tell the whole story. Throughout the night, beneath the crude brush arbors, Southern surgeons treat the wounded and dying on operating tables hammered together from rough-cut planks and posts. Nineteenth-century medical services haven't advanced much beyond bloodletting, and here in the woods of North Georgia conditions are horrible. Field hospitals have few, if any, pharmaceutical supplies. Because they lack antiseptics, infection and gangrene run rampant. Sanitation is awful. Improper latrines, bad drinking water, dirt, flies, and maggots seem to be everywhere. Overworked surgeons, baffled by the extent of the maiming and killing, make their diagnoses on hunches and prayers. Surrounded by suffering, they have only opium to administer as a painkiller. It's a wonder how the surgeons manage to save so many of the wounded. But they do.[10]

The field hospitals are crowded with not only casualties and medical personnel, but also with soldiers who are searching for their missing comrades. Well into the night, the wounded are carried to the hospitals by wagons, litters, or on the backs of fellow soldiers. Sam Watkins, First Tennessee Infantry, passes two men bearing a litter as he makes his way through the dark toward the front lines to meet his regiment. "Who have you there?" he asks. "Captain Asa G. Freeman," one of the men answers. Thus, Watkins suddenly learns that it's his uncle who is lying on their stretcher and solicitously asks if the wound is dangerous. "Shot through both thighs," they reply and continue on to the field hospital. Watkins, like any veteran, understands the seriousness of such wounds. Gunshots to the limbs typically lead to amputations, especially if the bone is shattered. And amputations can result in infection, an unwanted problem that can cause any wound to become fatal.[11]

The .58-caliber ball, loaded by dirty hands, contaminated with germs, and not moving through the air quite fast enough to be self-purifying, inflicts most of the battle wounds. On impact, the ball not only tears up flesh and bone, but also carries pieces of a dirty uniform with it into the wound. So went the ball that passed through one of the lungs of Sgt. Whit Phillips, Third Texas Cavalry, while fighting in an oak grove just west of the churchyard at New Hope. After reaching the hospital, the operating surgeon "laid him down on the table and cut out the big ball from the back and with the ball came a piece of leather strap, gunstring, and a piece of checked shirt that had passed with the ball through his body." In the days ahead, Phillips, a farmer before the war, suffers intensely but somehow manages to survive the ordeal and is sent back home to Texas.[12]

Many don't survive. Others are barely living but have given up hope, praying for death to hurry. They are the unfortunate ones who bare the grotesque wounds that surgeons don't bother to treat. Lower jaws, for instance, are sometimes shot away, exposing lolling tongues that can't call for help. Young boys and old men lie side by side, eviscerated by shot and shell, entrails hanging, bowels exposed, and twist in agony on their blankets as they whimper for their loved ones. To bring such horrors home takes an account from a battlefield witness. From a field hospital, two days after the battle of New Hope Church, Hiram Williams sadly enters in his diary his version of a soldier's death:

> The soldier is mortally wounded on the field, but not quite dead. He is borne on a litter to a safe position where the ambulances of his Brigade takes him to the Hospital. There the Doctor perhaps pronounces his case hopeless, and he is laid aside where he lingers for an hour, perhaps a day, then dies. If there is any hope his wound is dressed, then perhaps he dies after a day or so, and he meets a soldier's burial, in the same clothes in which he died, unwashed, smeared in his own gore—a horrid sight. We dig him a grave, two

feet deep, wrap him in his blanket, if he has one, and cover him up. Such is a soldier's burial at the hospital.[13]

As soon as the surgeon gives the nod, the orderlies will drag off another body for burial. There's no music, no eulogy, no one preaches, and by this stage of the war, the sight is so familiar that many of the men have grown callous and indifferent to death. Unfortunately, there are times when some poor wretch is mistakenly pronounced dead by the surgeon and hauled off for burial. Just such an occurrence takes place at New Hope Church when Pvt. R. J. McGowen, Thirty-seventh Alabama, is thrown on an ambulance and packed off to the hospital after being knocked unconscious by an exploding shell. After lying there comatose for several hours, someone decides McGowen is dead, and the orderlies drag him away for burial. "As they took him up to roll him in his blanket preparatory to laying him in his grave, he gave a kick, and he was laid down and in a few minutes was able to sit up. . . . A few minutes more to the horror of war would have been added that of being buried alive."[14]

Throughout the night, both sides attend to the wounded and bury their dead. It bears mentioning that Dan Butterfield, whose division was heavily engaged in the battle, is also a witness to the suffering and death. He is the composer of the bugle melody *Taps,* a tune he had written two years earlier on a Virginia battlefield. It's conceivable, though not recorded, that somewhere during the dark of this night one of his buglers, in the customary tribute to the fallen, blows the tune again. The notes are melancholy, almost haunting, drifting through the woods around New Hope Church and finding the ears of Union and Confederate alike:

Fading light . . . falling night
Trumpet calls as the sun sinks in flight
Sleep in peace comrade dear
God is near.[15]

Chapter Six

But the Ditch! Oh, What an Experience

The scent of rain is still in the air when the gray dawn breaks on Thursday morning, May 26, 1864. The new day reveals long lines of entrenched soldiers, blue and gray, zigzagging for miles over damp, wooded ridges. Joe Johnston has spent the night at Hood's headquarters where he has made plans for today's battle. At present, the cautious Johnston is content to remain in a defensive posture. The only tactical change that will be made is on Hood's advice to extend and strengthen their right, as the big Kentuckian believes Sherman will move eastwardly and attempt to rejoin the railroad. To meet this threat, Johnston detaches Pat Cleburne's division from Hardee's corps, now in the vicinity of Dallas, and sends it to bolster Hood's right.[1] It goes without saying that Johnston would welcome another attack on one of his fortified positions, resulting in another defensive victory such as yesterdays under A. P. Stewart, with whom he is well pleased. So pleased, in fact, that Stewart will soon find himself promoted to lieutenant general. That position will become available in less than three weeks when Bishop Polk is blown nearly in half by a Union artillery shell. Although Stewart's record is a good one, the promotion will be at least partly in recognition for his defiant stand at New Hope Church. However, Old Straight is a modest man, refusing to crow over his feats, and only years later does he admit that the battle on May 25 was among "the most noteworthy incidents in my war career."[2]

This same morning finds Sherman reconsidering any plans he may have had for an early attack. As soon as there's light enough, he sees "a strong line of intrenchments facing us, with a heavy force of infantry and guns."[3] Now he must bring up all his forces, deploying Thomas and Schofield in the area facing New Hope

Church and lengthen his line (as Hood had predicted) toward the railroad. McPherson's corps, in the meantime, must be brought up to the town of Dallas and its line extended eastwardly so as to connect with Thomas's right. This junction, however, will not be made for days, and a mile-long gap soon appears between McPherson's left and Thomas's right, a situation that will continue to trouble Sherman in the days to come. Likewise, the Confederate line fails to join Hardee's right with Polk's left, temporarily creating a similar breach. Since the thick, tangled woods hide these gaps, neither side is able to take advantage of them.[4]

Sherman is frustrated. This sudden Rebel resistance has complicated matters, upset his plans, and thrown his army into disorder, all of which grates on his nerves. It will surprise him when he learns that he's facing Johnston's entire army, and surprise is never a welcomed event in war, especially for someone like Sherman who constantly strives for order and purpose in his life. Adding to the unexpected appearance of a fortifying enemy, he's annoyed with the junglelike terrain that surrounds his army. Wiring Gen. Henry Halleck in Washington, he complains that the "country [is] very densely wooded and broken" and that there are "no roads of any consequence."[5] What's more, he's wrathy over an increasing number of stragglers wandering through the woods toward the rear, presumably in search of something to eat. This, of course, gives him another opportunity to light into Hooker. "I find a perfect string of men going back for rations," he scolds him. Blaming him that they don't have three days' rations in their haversacks as ordered, he rails on, "I don't want any more men to the rear. I will turn everybody back. This is an order and is peremptory . . . be ready for battle." All of these woes give Sherman cause to agree with his troops when he overhears them calling this new battleground the "Hell-Hole."[6]

****

Indeed, the description "Hell-Hole" is already living up to its name. Two huge armies, like beasts glaring at each other, have drawn their lines in a primitive, lonesome forest. Between these lines, only one hundred yards apart in some places, the woods are in ruins where Stewart and Hooker's divisions have already clashed. Scythed by artillery fire, the trees have been torn down or splintered, leaving the ground strewn with the debris from their trunks, limbs, and foliage. In this area, where the destruction of the forest was heaviest, the lines are now within sight of each other, and the tangled ground between them becomes a killing ground where soldiers dare not venture. In the days to come, the Hell Hole will serve as a preview for the miserable trench warfare of World War I, which is still fifty years in the future. Another time, another place, but the wretched conditions at Ypres in the Belgian province of Flanders will bear a morbid similarity to the madness here in the woods of North Georgia. Both are scenes of muddy ditches, separated by a no-man's land, where men will live and die like wild animals. The difference here is that these are not foreigners facing each other. These are Americans, some of them related, who speak the same language, read the same Bible, and share the same heritage. Thus, we find farm boys from Iowa and Mississippi staring at each other from their ditches across a vine-clogged land, wondering what God intends to happen here.

With the lines falling into place, work commences on the breastworks and continues until some of them become quite elaborate. Typically, the ditches are fairly wide and dug about three feet deep with the excavated dirt being thrown over logs piled in front of the ditches, forming what is known as a parapet. Heaped on top of all of this they place a head log or huge tree trunk supported by skid poles extending across the width of the ditch. If the head log happens to be hit by an artillery shell, the poles will allow it to roll toward the back of the ditch instead of falling on the men. The skid poles also create an embrasure or gap from which the men can fire their weapons with at least some degree of safety. To discourage an attack, the more enterprising soldiers also construct abatis in which brush is dragged in front of the parapet and branches or saplings are sharpened and pointed toward the enemy. Finally, so as not to obscure their vision, they clear away the underbrush in front of the breastworks to create a killing field.[7]

From these breastworks, both armies routinely send out pickets and skirmishers, creeping into the no-man's land between their

Confederate breastworks at New Hope Church, from The Photographic History of the Civil War, *1911, 3:113*

respective works. The soldiers hug the ground, lying flat behind whatever cover they can find and hope to be relieved before one of the enemy's bullets can find them. It's unpleasant duty but necessary in order to alert the main line to an enemy charge and to protect the men who are constantly working to improve their breastworks. "Skirmish and picket duty is by far the most risky of any," claims Spillard F. Horral, Forty-second Indiana Regiment. In some areas, the opposing pickets are only fifty yards apart and exposed to the spattering of rifle fire, which continues both day and night. Several times a day "the picket firing is as sharp as in pitched battle." It's dangerous business when the time comes to substitute the pickets. "Impossible," declares Horral, "to relieve them without bringing on a sharp fight." Accomplishing this is obviously more successful when night falls, but even then, the snapping of a twig or a kicked stone will ignite another uproar of the enemy's rifle fire.[8]

While their breastworks provide some safety, they also prove to be somewhat of an ordeal for the soldiers. "But the ditch! Oh what an experience," wails Horral. "To get out of the ditch on high ground, with the enemy pickets so near is almost certain death by day-time and little less so in the night-time," he grumbles. However, remaining in the ditch brings on other miseries. The rain has been intermittently pouring on them since Wednesday evening and will continue to fall. It fills the ditches, leaving the men standing "ankle to knee deep" in mud and water. Anyone not on picket duty is "busy bailing out the water." As exhaustion sets in, the men become desperate to get some sleep, causing Horral to ask the rhetorical question: "Would you think it possible under such conditions?" Then he concedes that when the urge finally overwhelms them, the "men slept sitting, standing, kneeling, and every way except lying down." Also, fires for cooking or warmth are usually impossible because of the wet conditions and the likelihood that they will provide targets for enemy gunners. So lacking the means to cook, the men resort to the hardtack or any of the cold commissary rations they can get their hands on.[9]

Here, civilized men are turned into troglodytes, crawling and wallowing in the muddy pits, afraid to show themselves. From the ditches, "we could plainly see the Confederate works during the day," remarks Cpl. John Clemson, Forty-sixth Ohio, "and no man dare raise his head above the works lest it become a target for watchful sharpshooters."[10] These sharpshooters are constantly on the lookout for a bobbing head, and some of their high-powered weapons, such as a Whitworth, can blow that head off from a half-mile away. Texas private Henry Lacy overhears one man close to him bragging, "I am going to kill me a Yankee as soon as I eat this bread." Finishing his meal, the man throws his rifle over the head log and waits a few seconds. Then he quickly raises his head over the log and fires. Suddenly it becomes apparent that a Yankee sniper has been watching, waiting for the head to follow the rifle, and in that split second, Lacy watches in horror as a ball strikes the bread-eater in the forehead, "scattering his brains in every direction." According to Lacy, the man never spoke, but he found it "strange that the victim lived two hours in this condition."[11]

Incidents such as this one begin to cause apprehension and worry among the soldiers. Everyone knows that they could be next, like William Norrell, a Georgia private, whose diary entry for May 26 includes the anxious words "dread to think of what we may experience today or before we get from this field."[12] In the days and nights to follow, the dread and nervous tension will only worsen, causing some to break down emotionally under the strain. Others will pretend to be sick, slinking off to the field hospitals or hiding in the rear. A few will risk the provost guards and desert in the night. But the great majority will find ways to cope with their fears and to bear grimly the dangers and miseries of the ditches. Many of them, such as J. P. Cannon and his fellow Alabamians, just try to make the best of it; "amusing ourselves by shooting at the Yanks every time we could see one and getting shot at when we dared to raise our heads above the breastworks." To "lay low," as Cannon puts it, they can usually avoid harm, "except occasionally when a fragment of shell would strike some poor fellow who was unfortunate enough to have made his bed in an unlucky spot." But leaving the ditch is an altogether different matter. Those chosen for the dangerous detail of bringing back water or supplies will "draw the fire of hundreds of guns from the opposite side and although quite serious to them, sometimes it is right amusing to see them run and dodge until they get shelter behind a hill or so far into the timber they cannot be seen."[13]

Besides watching the spectacle of some poor soul running for his life, they entertain themselves just as soldiers have all through the ages. During the lulls in the firing when boredom overtakes them, the literate ones reread old letters and pen new ones. Others gamble with greasy cards or clean their weapons, and everyone curses the war. With the lines so close together, it's not unusual for conversations to break out between them. "Occasionally the pickets, which are within hailing distance, will suspend their fire, and hold a short discourse with each other," writes Maj. Lewis D. Warner, 154th New York. Usually these chats are in "the blackguard order," reviling one another, but often end up "with 'take care rebels, or yank' when bang goes the musket, and the conference is at an end, and each looks out for his own head."[14]

Even in war, it seems there are times when the soldiers just can't hide their social nature. Friendly talks with the enemy, however, are temporary at best. Confederate private Bob Goodlet, for instance, brings the firing to a complete stop when he lures a glib-tongued Yankee into a conversation about swapping newspapers. Goodlet, obviously an amiable sort, convinces the Yankee spokesman to meet him halfway between the lines and make the swap. This probably sounds like a fine idea to the soldiers, who could use an unread newspaper—even one of the enemy's. Apparently, the Yankee officers don't agree and forbid any such nonsense when they realize a liaison with a Rebel is about to occur. However, by now Goodlet is over the breastworks and strutting toward the hostile lines to claim that paper. Nothing is left for the Yankee negotiator to do but climb atop his own breastworks and yell, "Go back Johnny Reb, they won't let me." Instantly bullets fill the air, and poor Goodlet runs for his life, diving back into his ditch in just a nick of time. It's a close call, bringing them back to the grim reality of the ditches.[15]

The day passes without either side attempting any significant offensive movement. Brief sorties do occur when one side or the other launches a line of skirmishers, usually to drive enemy pickets away from their breastworks. For the most part, however, these are isolated clashes, and over most of the long lines, the soldiers simply watch and wait and continue their diggings. Soon the air begins to fill with the sickening stench of the decomposing bodies of unburied men and dead horses lying in the thicket in front of New Hope Church. "Almost intolerable," gags Indiana trooper Henry Perry, "no wonder the boys named it the Hell Hole." Confederate private Sam Watkins agrees in disgust, grumbling, "We had to breathe the putrid atmosphere."[16]

Perhaps William Nugent, a Mississippi captain, best describes the essence of life in the ditches when he sums up the experience in a letter to his wife:

Mud, filth, rain; every imaginable species of vermin crawling all around you; little sleep, hard work & fed like a race horse; constantly annoyed with stray bullets, whizzing shells and pattering grape; dirty clothes and not a change along; little or no time to wash your face and hands and very little soap when the opportunity offers.

Undoubtedly, he speaks for thousands when he tells her, "How I would like to be five thousand miles from here now."[17]

Sherman, too, would like to be far away from this place. What little patience he has is wearing thin as he watches this new trench warfare developing. At the end of the day, he issues his orders for tomorrow, which he hopes will extract him from these miserable ditches and move his army forward. At first light, he wants every piece of artillery that Hooker, Howard, and Schofield can bring up to open fire, blasting the Confederate ditches from one end to the other. At 10:00 A.M., Oliver Howard's corps, supported by two divisions from the XXIII Corps, will swing around the Rebels' right flank, where he will attack them at some point northeast of New Hope Church. Meanwhile, McPherson, from the Dallas area, "will move straight toward the enemy, and make connection with General Hooker's right." Thus Sherman intends to hammer away at both flanks of whatever force is in his front, although he's still not exactly sure what that force is.[18]

Chapter Seven

Why Don't They Stop Those
Damned Bugles?

Just as Sherman has commanded, sunrise on Friday brings the roar of Union cannon and, as expected, a booming reply from the Confederate's big guns. The new day also brings a weather change. The rain, at least for the time being, has stopped, and the Georgia air turns humid and sultry. Sometime during the night, Gen. William Hardee, commanding the Confederate left, receives intelligence alerting him that McPherson is preparing for a change in his position, which, as one of Hardee's staff later recalls, "necessitated new dispositions on our part."[1] And so at 3:00 A.M., the divisions of Frank Cheatham and W. H. T. Walker are awakened and redeployed to counter the Federal movement. At daylight on May 27, James McPherson, following Sherman's orders, begins probing the Confederate left flank where his troops quickly become tangled up in heavy skirmishing all along Hardee's line. The fighting is especially heavy between Cheatham's division and elements of the Union XV Corps, both struggling for possession of Elsberry Ridge, a low rise crossing the Villa Rica Road below New Hope Church. By late morning, McPherson becomes convinced that the Rebel left flank is too strong to drive back or turn as Sherman had hoped. After learning this, Sherman sends a note to McPherson at 11:00 A.M., "If you can't drive the enemy from his position, work to your left, so as to connect with Hooker." But McPherson can't move to his left or, for that matter, anywhere else without exposing his flank to attack. In effect, he is pinned down, and the skirmishing and demonstrations will continue on his front throughout this day and for days to come.[2]

A few miles to the east, as the warm dawn breaks on Friday morning, the men of Gen. Thomas J. Wood's division have just put the finishing touches on their breastworks. Early in the day,

Wood is informed by his corps commander, Oliver Howard, of Sherman's plan to strike both the Confederate flanks and that his division has been chosen for the "arduous and dangerous task . . . to find the extreme right of the enemy's position, turn it, and attack him in flank."[3] Howard goes on to explain that Richard W. Johnson's division of the XIV Corps will support him in this dangerous mission. Wood, on the other hand, is not especially happy with his new assignment. After all, his men have worked throughout the night preparing some very stalwart breastworks, and in the process, some of them were killed. Now another division, Gen. David Stanley's, will enjoy the protection of their labor and sacrifice while they are ordered into harm's way. But such is war, and Wood will obey his orders.[4]

Wood's men begin crawling from the safety of their breastworks a little after 8:00 A.M., but according to Howard's adjutant, it's nearly 11:00 A.M. before they finally begin their movement. That delay results when Howard and his superior, George Thomas, reconnoiter the ground over which they are to advance and suddenly realize the men must pass through an open field where they would be exposed to "murderous direct and cross fire" from enemy artillery. After seeing this, the two generals decide to change the planned direction of attack, choosing instead a safer route where the division will swing to the rear of John Schofield's line now occupying the army's left and attempt to come around the Confederate right flank. They move out with Howard and his staff accompanying Wood's division and Richard Johnson's division following on their left.[5]

The men soon discover that while this new route may be less hazardous, it's also an extremely difficult course for them to maneuver. They are forced to claw their way through thickly covered woods and tangled underbrush, up and down an endless succession of hills and ravines. Traveling under these conditions, officers are forced to rely on pocket compasses for direction. Brigade commanders, trying to communicate and guide their troops, break silence and resort to signaling each other with bugles. "Nothing could be seen ahead," complains Sgt. Gregory McDermott. "It was like groping in the darkness, and the old bugle sounded ahead, I suppose to guide us, but we objected to it on account of it attracting the Johnnies' shells so often, for every now and then one would burst overhead, breaking the branches of the trees and causing a scattering." Another strenuous objector to the blaring bugles is Lt. Alexis Cope, who agrees with the men when they complain, "If we are expected to surprise the enemy, why don't they stop those damned bugles?"[6]

As the blue columns plod eastward seeking the Confederates' flank, Howard stops them periodically and orders skirmishers to the south, feeling for the end of Joe Johnston's long gray line. Shortly before two in the afternoon, after traveling a mile and a half, Howard halts them again. "I thought we must have reached the enemy's flank," he recalls. But when his skirmishers move forward they find an open field, beyond which they see the familiar pilings of red Georgia dirt, indicating still more Rebel breastworks. So they trudge on. Nearing 4:00 P.M., after covering another mile or so, one-armed Howard is satisfied he must be past their flank. He stops to rest the troops, who are nearly worn out by now, and he and Wood ride forward to confirm the supposition that they are finally past the enemy's right. "We still found a line of works to our right," Howard moans in frustration. These diggings, however, "were new, the enemy still working hard upon them." Furthermore, he's encouraged that he can finally see what he believes to be the end of the Rebel breastworks and decides to make his move here.[7]

Howard orders Wood and Johnson to turn their divisions to the south in preparation to attack. On the hope that he's right, he scribbles a note to George Thomas, headed 4:35 P.M., and sends it by a colonel on his staff.

> General: I am on the ridge beyond the field that we were looking at this morning. No person can appreciate the difficulty in moving over this ground unless he can see it. I am on the east side of the creek which Pickett's Mill is, facing south, and am now turning the enemy's right flank, I think.[8]

Whatever reaction Thomas or Sherman may have had to Howard's trailing remark—*I think*—is not recorded. Ordinarily, Sherman would redden at such an admission of uncertainty and vacillation from one of his corps commanders. In this instance, it's likely that the fiery red-haired general understands and appreciates Howard's present dilemma, as evident in a note he sends to Schofield about this same time. "It is useless to look for the flank of the enemy," he concedes, "as he makes temporary breastworks as fast as we travel." In any case, Howard's staff colonel quickly returns telling him, "General Thomas says that Major General Sherman wishes us to get on the enemy's right flank and rear as soon as possible." Even though it's obvious that Sherman is anxious for the attack to begin, the point where they strike the enemy is becoming less important to him than the urgency of getting on with the attack. He makes that desire clear in his message to Schofield, "We must break his line, without scattering our troops too much, and then break through."[9]

Howard peers through his binoculars studying the enemy's freshly dug breastworks and the washboard ground over which his men must pass. Known as Pickett's Mill, the land is like everything else around it, rolling from one rocky ridge to the next, separated by ravines, and all covered with big timber that shades a tangled undergrowth of brush and saplings. From what Howard understands, most of the land is owned by the widow Martha Pickett, known simply to her friends and family as Fanny. At twenty-seven years old, with four children, she seems too young to be known as the Widow Pickett, except here in the South where widows and orphans are becoming the norm and a common sight. Her husband, Benjamin, a lieutenant in the Confederate army, has been taken from her, killed last September at Chickamauga. With his death, she inherits a three-hundred-acre farm and a gristmill powered by the small creek that runs through the property and bears their name. She seldom encounters anyone she doesn't know, and suddenly she finds herself surrounded by thousands of strangers, soldiers traipsing through her woods and blowing bugles. Something like this doesn't happen everyday on the farm, and, like her neighbors, she and her family have become refugees, forced to flee from their home.[10]

With the exception of a couple of small wheat fields, a cornfield, and the areas around the gristmill and farmhouse, there are few clearings in the Widow Pickett's dark, beguiling woods. The battlefield to be is shaped somewhat like a triangle, bounded on the east by the northward flowing Pickett's Creek, sometimes called Little Pumpkin Vine Creek. At its northern apex, the creek meets the straight road running southwest to the town of

Dallas. That road forms the western boundary of the triangle and eventually crosses the ridgeline where the Rebels have continued to entrench. Rambling along the ridge, in an eastward direction, and back to the creek completes the geometry, providing the base or south line for the battlefield.

Into the center of this deadly triangle, Howard orders Wood to place his division in columns of brigades, just as Hooker had employed his formation at New Hope Church. As ordered, Wood deploys his three brigades, placing William B. Hazen's in front, followed by William H. Gibson's, and finally Frederick Knefler's. On their left, Richard Johnson is slowly moving his division through briar and bramble down and across the opposite side of Pickett's Creek, with Benjamin Scribner's brigade leading the way. However, they are still too far back to properly support Wood's left. Over on the right, Nathaniel McLean's brigade from Schofield's XXIII Corps, and now assigned to Howard, is ordered to occupy a cleared area where, according to plan, he is supposed to announce his presence by demonstrating and diverting attention away from the main attack.[11]

* * * * * * * * * * * * * *

Having deployed his troops, Oliver Howard is growing more skeptical by the minute. He's still unsure over the enemy's strength and actual position. According to a captured Rebel, the Confederate divisions of both Patrick Cleburne and Thomas Hindman are dug in somewhere beyond the thick timber in front of him. The truth is, however, the Rebels in his path are solely from Cleburne's division, which Johnston had dispatched from Hardee's corps around Dallas on the morning of May 26 well before sunrise. They traveled all day, moving up the Mount Tabor Road and following the sounds of sporadic rifle fire from Sherman's lines that continued crawling eastward. Finally, they met and passed Hindman's division of Hood's corps, which until then had been the end of Johnston's line. That afternoon Cleburne's men continued on to the Pickett's Mill settlement, where they have anchored on the extreme right of the Confederate army.[12]

James McPherson (Courtesy Prints and Photographs Division, Library of Congress)

George Thomas (Courtesy Prints and Photographs Division, Library of
Congress, LC-B8172-6480)

If Howard had been able to pick which of the enemy's divisions, Cleburne or Hindman, he would prefer to tangle with, it surely would not have been Cleburne's. They are perhaps the best Johnston has to offer. Hard-bitten veterans of the Army of Tennessee, they have fought in nearly all its campaigns. And a mean bunch they are. Under Cleburne's leadership, these wild roughnecks from Texas and backwoodsmen from Arkansas have been disciplined into a fierce and spirited fighting unit. A model division, their *esprit de corps* rivals that of any in the army. Because of a great fighting record, Joe Johnston has allowed them to continue marching under their distinctive dark blue flags centered with a white or silver moon while the rest of the army carries the standard battle flag bearing the cross of St. Andrews.[13]

When Cleburne's boys start streaming onto the ridges near Pickett's Mill they aren't sure what their mission will be or, for that matter, even where they are. "We don't know whether we are on the right, left or centre of the army," admits Capt. Sam Foster, Twenty-fourth Texas. What they do know is that they are there to fight, which is evident to them by the heavy firing "on our left and front all day today." Curious as to what other Confederates might be in the area, Foster says,

> Some of our boys go to the breastworks in front of us to see what soldiers are there, because they have no confidence in any of them except the Arkansas troops. We find Georgia troops in our front; and our boys tell them that if they run that we will shoot them, and no mistake, and as soon as they find out that the Texans are in their rear, they believe we will shoot them sure enough.[14]

Finding they are alone, the surly veterans begin throwing up breastworks and digging rifle pits. The next day, May 27, as Howard's men are groping their way through the thicket toward Pickett's Mill, Cleburne's men are not only ensconced, but, thanks to "those damned bugles," have an excellent idea of their enemy's whereabouts.

Chapter Eight

The Strong Fine Soul Within

At first glance, thirty-six-year-old Patrick Ronayne Cleburne does not look the part of a general who will command men in battle. Most physical accounts describe him as a tall, lanky-framed, and awkward man with a somewhat plain almost homely visage. He has the cold, distant look of a loner, a man with few close friends. By this point in the war, he has grown a skimpy beard and mustache in an attempt to cover an ugly scar around his mouth, the reminder of a Yankee bullet that had blown out two of his front teeth, causing a hissing sound in his speech when he isn't careful. Another bullet found him at the battle of Perryville, where he was hit in the lower leg, and has left him with a slight limp. When New York newspaperman David Conyngham sees Cleburne in one of those rare, after-battle truces, he writes, "I saw Pat Cleburne, with that tall, meager frame, and that ugly scar across his lank, gloomy face, stand with a thoughtful air, looking on the work his division had done. . . . He looked a fit type of the lean Cassius." But beneath his plain and damaged façade, there is something more to Pat Cleburne, something an Arkansas private is insightful enough to sense: "There was but one redeeming feature in his face, and that was his eye! An eye worth noticing. Earnest, thoughtful, grave, those clear grey orbs let out something of the strong fine soul within."[1]

Cleburne is an Irish immigrant who, at the young age of twenty-three, shows up in Arkansas with not much more than the shirt on his back and a burning desire to succeed. He begins his life in America as a drugstore clerk and eventually becomes a respected lawyer with large land holdings and another of our country's remarkable success stories. Although he never attends West Point, he lives as close to the code of ethics taught there (duty, honor,

Patrick Cleburne (Courtesy Prints and Photographs Division, Library of Congress, LC-USZ62-107446)

and country) as any of its graduates. But even without the benefit of a military education, he is a natural in the business of war. So good, in fact, that he will ultimately earn the moniker "Stonewall of the West."

A man of many virtues, Cleburne is admired for being honest, patient, considerate, and courageous, with an unbending sense of loyalty. He's not especially religious but has little use for drinking, smoking, swearing, and gambling, the usual soldierly vices. In Cleburne's pragmatic world, it's all black and white, where principles and values are never compromised. Ironically, these qualities proved to be a burden to him during the political upheaval of a country torn apart by war. His brutal honesty, for instance, is often offensive to fellow generals and alarming to Southern politicians. Just as he had been candid in his low estimate of Bragg, neither did he make a secret of his opinion of slavery, which was one of total indifference. "I never owned a Negro and care nothing for them," he wrote in a letter to his brother, Robert. What he does care about though is the ideal of Southern independence, for which he has dedicated himself to with a passion. As an immigrant, Cleburne never really understands or appreciates how the institution of slavery should be such a significant matter when compared to the more important issue of political freedom for the South. That naïve misunderstanding will prove to be his biggest mistake.[2]

Back in January, before the start of the Atlanta Campaign, Cleburne shocked the Confederacy's hierarchy when he proposed emancipating slaves and turning them into soldiers for the South. In a council of high-ranking officers, he explained how this would solve their manpower problem and, at the same time, deny the North of that very same resource, which by then they had already begun to tap. In Cleburne's mind, it was the only workable solution. In a lengthy argument, he had confronted them with a sober choice. "Between the loss of independence and the loss of slavery, we assume that every patriot will freely give up the latter—give up the Negro slave rather than be a slave himself." If Cleburne's proposal suggested any moral consideration, it was merely fortuitous because his primary objective was nothing more than a commonsense approach to the harsh reality of their problem. Nevertheless, when his plan became known in

Richmond, it was received with harrumphs and harangues from the politicians there who denounced the very idea as treasonous. Jefferson Davis quickly sent out a gag order, and Cleburne bit his tongue, suffered in silence, and never mentioned it again. How much this had damaged his military career is uncertain. But the fact remains that after his unpopular proposal, coupled with his earlier criticism of Bragg, Cleburne will be passed over for promotion on four different occasions.[3]

The disappointment Cleburne experienced over the rejection of his audacious proposal is somewhat mitigated by the success of a second proposal that he was hastily making about this same time. This time it was marriage. Before now, no one could have imagined Cleburne bringing himself to the romantic point of proposing marriage. He had never been known as a lady's man and was in fact "very bashful," according to his friend and biographer Charles Nash, who had seen the Irishman paralyzed in the presence of young women and noted "he blushed if one of them spoke to him."[4] But that was before he met Susan Tarleton, a twenty-four-year-old, pretty little blonde from Mobile, Alabama.

* * * * * * * * * * * * * * *

The two had met on January 13, 1864, at the wedding of Cleburne's corps commander, William J. Hardee, and Mary Foreman Lewis of Marengo County, Alabama. The opulent affair was held at Bleak House Plantation near Demopolis. Cleburne served as Hardee's best man and Susan was maid of honor for the bride. Here, the officers in their best-dress uniforms escorted ladies attired in elegant dresses through a mansion rich with mahogany furniture, fine carpets, and expensive paintings. Elite, highbrow folks from Alabama's best families crowded through the parlors and halls. For everyone, it was a gathering that recalled a time of affluence, a throwback to those delicate and civilized days before the South had been nearly devastated by war. Cleburne was especially enjoying the moment, and he was infatuated with Susan Tarleton, never leaving her side. For him, it was a different world, and he had nearly forgotten how to act in such a proper setting. After all, this was the first time in more than two years that he had been away from his men. Now he's dazed by the grandness of such a festive celebration, far removed from the ordeal of leading his bunch of ragged, barefooted boys through the endless and impossible fights.[5]

After the ceremony, the wedding party boarded a paddle-wheel steamboat for a romantic cruise down the Tombigbee River to Mobile. This was just too much for the Irishman's emotions, and by the next day when the boat docked, he was hopelessly in love with "Miss Sue." In Mobile, Cleburne checked into the Battle House Hotel and spent the rest of his furlough calling on her at the family home at 351 St. Louis Street. Susan Tarleton must have been impressed when the *Mobile Daily Advertiser and Register* carried several articles lauding her new beau for his war heroics. However, she still wouldn't consent to his first marriage proposal, which he had made before leaving to rejoin his troops in North Georgia. Nevertheless, he returned six weeks later more determined than ever. This time she agreed to marry him. A pleasing change came over Cleburne who, ever since making his first proposal, had claimed to be "miserable." Elated that she had accepted him, he writes a friend, "After keeping me in cruel suspense for six weeks, she has at length consented to be mine and we are engaged." What Cleburne doesn't know, because he cannot, is that Susan Tarleton, like the Arkansas private, has been able to look beyond the quiet, shy countenance and the scarred face to see "the strong fine soul within."[6]

✼✼✼✼✼✼✼✼✼✼✼✼✼✼✼✼

The wedding, of course, must wait on the war that drags on through the Atlanta Campaign, reducing the romance to the reading and writing of long love letters. But that too is now interrupted by the savage fighting around New Hope Church. Cleburne must now turn his attention to the two Yankee divisions bearing down on the Army of Tennessee's right flank. Early on the morning of May 27, he orders Daniel Govan's brigade to conduct a reconnaissance, moving first north then swinging to the left to determine the enemy's whereabouts and strength. Govan's constant reports validate Cleburne's suspicions that Howard is continuing to move, trying to skirt around their flank. Since he is now reporting to Hood for his orders, Cleburne asks the general's permission to extend his division farther to the east to meet this threat. At 9:50 A.M., Hood replies in a note sent by courier that he's free to do so "provided the movement can be made without attracting special attention from the enemy." Thus, at 11:00 A.M., Cleburne brings Govan's brigade back into line and sends them sidling to the east of Lucius Polk's brigade, which until now had been on the extreme right of his division.[7]

This same morning, Hiram Granbury, a Texas lawyer now commanding one of Cleburne's brigades, orders a scouting party into the woods on still another fact-finding mission. They are instructed to circumvent the Yankee column and pinpoint their exact location. As the Texans make their way through the dense forest, they stumble on the Widow Pickett's farmhouse, which is empty, the family apparently having fled as the sounds of battle drew closer. Before leaving, however, they took the time to hide some of their valuables. The men notice that an old well has been crammed full with household goods, including a featherbed. The group of scouts continues on its mission, finally returning that afternoon and reporting that the enemy "were massing their troops on the right of our army and would flank us before night if we did not stop them some way." After hearing this, Cleburne is forced to leapfrog another of his brigades to the right, this time ordering Granbury, who had previously been in reserve, to take up a position on Govan's right.[8]

By 4:00 P.M., three of Cleburne's four veteran brigades are in battle position with Granbury's brigade nearly there as they hurriedly file past Govan's troops. Lucius Polk, nephew of corps commander Bishop Polk and one of Cleburne's few close friends, anchors the left. To his right, Cleburne tucks in an Alabama battery of howitzers, napoleons, and parrot guns facing nearly due north. Next in line is Daniel Govan's Arkansas brigade, dug into rifle pits on a ridge that looks down on a wheat field in the ravine below. At this point, where a sharp spur juts northeastwardly from the ridge, Cleburne instructs Thomas Key to haul two pieces of artillery up a steep slope to a "convenient breach made in our breastworks" between the brigades of Govan and Granbury. They are placed frowning down into the ravine to achieve an enfilading fire. The only troops east of Granbury's brigade are some eight hundred dismounted cavalry under Gen. John Kelly and Gen. William Hume, both brigadiers from Joe Wheeler's command. Their line runs off in a northeast direction from a point near the cornfield on Granbury's right and prolongs Cleburne's line along a rocky ridge that borders the creek. The last of Cleburne's brigades, commanded by Mark Lowery, is set back in a reserve position behind Granbury and just north of the road leading to New Hope Church.[9]

Cleburne, now as always, is concerned with preparations. Mounted on his big bay, Red Pepper, he rides the wooded ridge inspecting his lines. He's a stickler for details, and none escape him. From experience, he knows that he will probably be outnumbered, and by now, he's hardened to facing that same old problem. He understands he can leave nothing to chance. The woods are thick, and he knows it will be difficult moving men from one area to the next should he be forced to reinforce at any point up and down the line. Determined not to lose the day because of this, he sends his pioneers wading into the brush, hacking out paths, connecting the rear of one brigade with the next and so on to the end of the line. The crude network of trails will allow his troops the flexibility to move quickly through the bramble should an emergency arise. Continuing to make ready for an attack, he orders more ammunition brought up for his sharpshooters armed with deadly Whitworth rifles. He knows those weapons will be needed, and thanks to constant drilling, Cleburne's marksmen are the best trained in the army when it comes to using them.[10]

With his brigades deployed as ordered, Cleburne watches as the last of Granbury's troops take up their positions on the ridge. Among them is Capt. Sam Foster, who remarks, "Our position is in a heavy timbered section with chinquapin bushes for an undergrowth. From the end of the army, where the breastworks stop we followed a small trail or mill path and as soon as our Brigade got its whole length in this place the command is to halt." No sooner had they stopped than Foster sees some of Kelly's cavalry skirmishers come running through the woods in wild-eyed fright "saying that we had better get away from there, for they were coming by the thousand." Granbury's veterans, however, have no intention of running and begin crouching behind trees or piling up rocks for cover as they await the attack.[11]

Chapter Nine

The Criminal Blunder

While Cleburne's veterans fill the wooded ridges and hills overlooking the Pickett Settlement, Union lieutenant Ambrose Bierce is creeping through the woods below, inching his way toward the Rebel lines. Bierce, at twenty two years old, is a topographical engineer who is given the duty of surveying the ground over which Howard's men will attack. Born in Horse Cave Creek, Ohio, the tenth of thirteen children of Marcus Aurelius and Laura Bierce, young Ambrose has grown up smothered in poverty and religion. His father, a dirt-poor, hardscrabble farmer, never had much success cultivating the land; in part, because he spent every spare cent he got his hands on buying books instead of plowshares and seed. Although investing in a library didn't do much for the elder Bierce, who is described as a "drab, dour, and plodding figure," it did open a door for his son to march through, allowing him to eventually take his place among the most gifted writers in American literature. But on this day in 1864, the future writer will witness an inhuman event that will shape his character and leave him cynically scarred by war as he discovers, in the words of one of his biographers, "how callous and casual high commanders could be about the lives of their men."[1]

After making what he calls a "hasty examination of the ground in front," Bierce quickly realizes that they will be forced to "march a quarter-mile uphill through almost impassable tangles of underwood, along and across precipitous ravines." Surrounded by wilderness and disoriented, Bierce, like Confederate Sam Foster and every other soldier present on either side, doesn't know what troops are on his left or his right, and knows very little about the enemy force in his front—"except," of course, "that it is unamiable." He also knows the Rebels are very close. From his forward scouting position, he has come far enough through the forest that from the next ridge he can "hear distinctly the murmur of the enemy awaiting us."[2]

Returning to the Union lines to report what he's seen and heard, Bierce finds his brigade already forming for battle. Assembling in columns, with two battalions in front and two in the rear, 1,500 men are quietly taking their places on a line some two hundred yards in width. Years later, he remembers the peace and stillness of the woods around them: "From our lines nothing could be heard but the wind among the trees and the songs of birds." The silence is occasionally broken by soft, nervous laughter as a few of the men restlessly joke among themselves. Overhearing the skittish soldiers, Bierce comments, "Men awaiting death on the battlefield laugh easily, though not infectiously."[3]

Bierce continues moving through the ranks until he finds Gen. William B. Hazen, his brigade commander, standing near his superiors, Generals Oliver Howard and Thomas Wood. Here is a trio of men who have all made mistakes during their military careers and have no desire to add another one on this day. Howard, in overall command, is hesitant to make the attack, fretting that a failure here would only add to his poor performances at Chancellorsville and Gettysburg. As shells begin to burst around them, he's convinced the Confederates know his position, and, according to a captured Rebel, they are waiting just ahead with the strength of two divisions. Even though Howard is the ranking general here, Thomas Wood will bear some scrutiny should the attack fail. Furthermore, much like Howard, he certainly wouldn't welcome another bad experience such as the one at Chickamauga. There Wood, a West Point, regular army, by-the-book kind of general, was simply following the orders of his commander, William Rosecrans, when he shifted his division, inadvertently opening a fatal breech in the blue lines that ultimately lost the day and the battle for the Union army. Rosecrans, in a rage, pointed straight at Wood, making him the scapegoat for the whole miserable affair.[4] Should a disaster occur here today, Sherman, too, might roll some heads, and Wood, in such case, would prefer that his not be among them.

Finally, there's William Hazen, commanding Wood's leading brigade, who Bierce describes as "the best hated man that I ever knew." Although Hazen is recognized as one of the most capable combat officers in the army, he's also earned the reputation throughout the ranks as hot-tempered and insubordinate. Ornery on his best days, he's clashed with both Grant and Sherman, incurred the wrath of the press, and has even challenged the secretary of war. "He was in trouble all around," as Bierce remembers. Yet, after so many campaigns together, the young lieutenant has grown to admire Hazen, calling his commander "my friend, my master in the art of war." He knows him as well as anyone, understands his many moods and complex character, portraying him as "aggressive, arrogant, tyrannical, honorable, truthful, courageous—a skillful soldier, a faithful friend, and one of the most exasperating of men."[5]

Heretofore, Hazen has been under the impression that the attack would be made in columns of brigades, much like Hooker's attack in front of New Hope Church. His brigade, as he understood the plan, would go in first, followed immediately by the other two in an attempt to overwhelm the Rebels with sheer numbers. "I learned this from his own lips," recounts Bierce. However, at 4:30 P.M., the very moment Hazen receives word to advance, he overhears Wood telling Howard, "We will put in Hazen and see what success he has." One-armed Howard is silent, simply nods at Wood in stoic approval. The remark is shocking news to Hazen, who is repulsed at the idea that his brigade will be thrown into the fray alone and unsupported. Also witnessing the exchange between commanders is Ambrose Bierce, who steals a quick glance at Hazen, anticipating an explosive reaction from his spunky general. But it doesn't come. "He never uttered a word," recalls Bierce. "Only by a look which I knew how to read did he betray his sense of the criminal blunder."[6]

"That, then, was the situation, a weak brigade of fifteen hundred men, with masses of idle troops behind in the character of an audience, waiting for the word to march," says Bierce.[7] Although small in number and going in alone, the men of Hazen's brigade are tough, seasoned veterans. The brigade, for the most part, is made up of Midwestern farm boys who aren't much different from Cleburne's troops waiting up on the ridge. Their attitudes, speech, and rough manners are similar. In fact, here in the woods of North Georgia, there are Kentuckians on both sides of the

William B. Hazen (Prints and Photographs Division, Library of Congress, LC-USZ62-104939)

contest. Granted, Hazen's boys probably wear a nicer uniform, enjoy better rations, and shoulder a superior weapon, but like their Rebel counterparts, they also know how to milk a cow, plow a mule, and slop a hog. Hardened by backbreaking farm lives, they are a different brand of Yankees than the ones who had struck Stewart's lines at New Hope Church. While those were veteran soldiers, some having formerly served with the Army of the Potomac, they were mostly easterners, city boys, and even some foreigners from New York or Pennsylvania, jabbering away in unfamiliar languages. After sizing up their foe, the prevailing opinion among the men of the Army of Tennessee is that the western Yankees now invading their homeland are a much harder strain of soldiers than those from the East.[8] In any case, here at Pickett's Mill, it's farm boy against farm boy, all tough, seasoned troops making ready to pitch into a horrible fight.

At the command, their feet rustle in the leaves as they move forward. Because of the tangled undergrowth, the officers send their horses to the rear and struggle alongside their men. Knowing their flags will be ripped to shreds by tree limbs and thorny vines, the color bearers keep them tightly wrapped around their staffs. As they move through the tangled thickets, the brigade quickly loses all shape of a formation, becoming nothing more than a mob. Lieutenant Bierce sees it as "simply a swarm of men struggling through the undergrowth of the forest, pushing and crowding." But Hazen's men are determined and continue to claw their way through the wooded ravine, stumbling and jumping over stumps and fallen trees, weaving through the bottoms and gullies, and splashing through the shallow creeks.[9]

Somewhere in the copse, the ravine takes off in a natural fork, causing the brigade to split left and right. The regiments that swarm down the steep sides of the left branch, mostly men from Kentucky and Indiana, suddenly find themselves pelted by fire from the dismounted Rebel cavalrymen who have moved down the slope of the ridge on the Confederate right. Bierce, among the Ohioans that have veered to the right, hears "the familiar hissing of bullets" and looks off to his left where "the interspaces of the forest were all blue with smoke." He remembers how "hoarse, fierce yells broke out of a thousand throats," as they begin to charge wildly through the woods, pushing back the gray skirmishers. Momentarily, the regiments on the left burst out into a clearing, the edge of a hollow where a cornfield begins. Crowding up against an old rail fence bordering the field, they drop to their knees, gasping for breath.[10]

Over on the right, the woods begin to explode around Hazen's troops. Pat Cleburne's well-placed batteries up on the ridge are finding their mark. Racket from the shots mingled with the screams of men and booming cannons are creating a deafening uproar. Bierce can't recall ever hearing such a violent clamor as he listens to the "gusts of grape . . . screaming among the trees." The Rebel artillery continues ripping the woods apart, splintering trees, sending chunks of earth flying, along with dozens of Hazen's men, tossed like rag dolls through the smoky air, arms and legs torn from their bodies. "We had, of course, no artillery to reply," recalls Bierce in a bitter afterthought.[11] And if there ever was a strategy, a battle plan, it's now forgotten. It's evolved into a two-pronged attack, with only Hazen's troops hitting a ridge along a two-hundred-yard front, most of which is occupied by Hiram Granbury's newly arrived Texas brigade.

Even though Oliver Howard sends only Hazen's brigade into the fight, he has believed, up until now, that they would be supported in flank by Richard Johnson's division on the left and on the right by a brigade borrowed from the XXIII Corps and commanded by Nathaniel McLean. At least that has been his impression. But so far, no one has seen a sign of either Johnson or McLean. Johnson knows what is expected of him, but he's been painfully slow getting his troops through the overgrown terrain beyond the creek and into position. They're still lagging back about a mile from where they should be, and Johnson is dithering, having second thoughts about making the attack. McLean, on the other hand, seems to have no apparent reason for not moving his troops. None, that is, except his hatred for Howard. Ever since he had been overrun by Stonewall Jackson's furious attack at Chancellorsville, Howard has blamed McLean, among others, for that disaster. And McLean, who was only a brigade commander there, is resentful of any such censure, resulting in a stone-cold relationship between the two men. The feud has continued, and McLean is steaming mad that he's found himself temporarily under Howard's command.

Despite receiving direct orders from Howard, he seems to have no intention of cooperating with that general's attack.[12]

The absence of Johnson and McLean on the flanks of Hazen's brigade is quickly setting the stage for a Union disaster. Now within one hundred yards of the Rebel lines, Hazen's left is resting at the edge of the cornfield where his panting Kentucky and Indiana troops are hugging a rail fence waiting for orders to advance. Kelly's dismounted cavalry continue to pelt them with fire from a ridge adjoining the creek. According to plan, Johnson's division should be protecting that flank but is tardy in arriving. Likewise, in jeopardy are the troops on Hazen's right who have just emerged from the thick woods into an area cleared by Cleburne's men as a killing ground. Suddenly, they find themselves under a murderous enfilading fire from Captain Key's Rebel artillery. Here the floor of the ravine begins its upward slope, and the men see that the only way out of the sweeping canister and solid shot from the Confederate cannons is to scramble up that rocky ridge. Off to their right is a wheat field where McLean's brigade should now be demonstrating and drawing at least some of the awful fire pouring down on them from the ridge. But the field is empty, and still there's no sign of McLean.

****

Up on the ridge, Granbury's Texans haven't had time to dig in or build breastworks, but they are well positioned behind rocks, stumps, and trees. From their cover come the sharp sounds of clicking metal, the cocking of gun hammers, followed by rapid gunfire, cracking up and down the lines. Four regiments of Ohio boys, their flags now unfurled, ascend the steep slope into what Hazen calls "one of the most desperate engagements of my experience." Hailstorms of lead fill the air as both sides are firing wildly, and everyone is yelling, cursing, and shouting at the top of their lungs. Taunting the wave of surging Yankees, a Rebel major hollers down at them, "Come on, we are demoralized," then falls to the ground, shot in the head. His wound, though not fatal, causes him some remorse, as he raises himself up and anxiously admits, "Boys, I told them a lie, and I believe that is the reason I got shot." Neither is there any shortage of jeering from the charging Yankees. "Ah! Damn you, we have caught you without your logs now," they scream while they continue to fire, clawing and dragging their way up the rocky ridge.[13]

Hazen's Ohioans finally force their way to within thirty yards of the Rebel lines where they find themselves on flatter ground, or what Cleburne later describes as a "natural glacis." Here, all hell breaks loose. The two sides stand frozen in a rage of fire. Blasting away from the higher ground, the Texans have the advantage, but Hazen's boys refuse to budge. From his position on the far right, Ambrose Bierce can look down the narrow space between the lines of blue and gray into what seems to be a smoke-filled alley of death. The firing is so deadly, so intense that it creates a phenomenon as ancient as warfare itself known to the soldiers as the *dead-line*. Through the dim smoke of the gantlet, Bierce watches as it takes shape "with its well-defined edge of corpses—those of the bravest. Where both lines are fighting without cover—as in a charge met by a counter-charge—each has its *dead-line* and between the two is a clear spot—neutral ground, devoid of dead, for the living cannot reach it to fall there" (emphasis added).[14]

Still some of Hazen's men manage to advance beyond the dead-line. They are the desperate ones who have given up hope of surviving where they stand. Falling back will only expose them to the crossfire they've just come through, but to stand their ground seems certain death. When their nerves reach the breaking point, they snap and lunge forward into that deadly space. In ones, twos, and small groups, they charge into the Rebel lines. Years later, Confederate sergeant A. G. Anderson remembers the reckless Yankee charges that day. "They seemed to be drunk, and line after line would charge us and be cut down. They came so close to us that they endeavored to plant their colors right in our lines, and when the flag would go down another man would raise it again. Many of their men rushed into our lines and were clubbed and bayoneted to death."[15]

The flag is of special importance for both sides. When their colors are flying, they feel undefeated, and the good soldiers can't bear to see theirs fall in the dirt. The color bearers are, of course, targets of choice and to capture an enemy flag will earn a man a medal. Here on the ridge, one of the Texas privates, William Oliphant, watches the Yankee color bearers shot down, one after another, as they try to keep their regimental banners flying. When the sixth man falls, still clutching the staff, he is within a few feet of the Rebel line. "There it lay, a prize within our grasp. I could have reached it with a single bound," Oliphant recalls. By now, however, the Yankee attack is beginning to crumble, their men falling back, and he decides to play it safe and "wait until their line had been completely driven back before picking it up." But as the Federals begin retreating down the slope, one young bluecoat throws down his gun, rushes back, and picks up the flag. "He straightened himself to his full height, gritted his teeth and flapped his flag in our faces." In a split second, Oliphant watches as "a half dozen rifles were leveled on him." Shortly, the insolent Yankee would be dead, but one of the Texans stops them from shooting, shouting, "Don't shoot him, he's too brave." At that, a loud cheer goes up, and the Rebels watch in admiration as he carries the flag back down the ridge.[16]

On Granbury's front, charge after charge meets with the same bloody result. But over on the Confederate right, Hazen's left wing is now in motion, spilling into the cornfield and threatening to overlap their flank. The only troops in front of them are Kelly's cavalrymen, who have been putting up a good fight but probably won't last much longer. Seeing a disaster unfolding before him, Granbury sends word to Daniel Govan for help. Govan reacts quickly and dispatches Col. George Baucam's Eighth/Nineteenth Consolidated Arkansas Regiment to plug the hole and drive back Hazen's charge. Passing to the rear of Granbury's brigade, they hightail it along the trails that Cleburne had wisely cut through the woods for just such an occasion as this and rush to the cornfield where Kelly's men are stubbornly hanging on.[17]

Knowing that more help will be needed to prolong his right, Cleburne sends couriers to bring up Gen. Mark Lowery's reserve brigade. Lowery, formerly a Baptist preacher from Mississippi and now serving the Almighty as a soldier under the Southern Cross, is moving his brigade toward the battle racket when he meets Pat Cleburne, weaving his horse through the trees and coming to meet him. The Irishman quickly explains the perilous situation to Lowery, telling him that Granbury is "hotly engaged" and that "the enemy had already passed to the rear of his right flank." As he listens, Lowery can't help but be impressed with Cleburne's cool composure in the heat of battle. "Move rapidly," Cleburne tells him in a calm voice, then adds, as he hastily rides away, "secure Granbury's right."[18]

****

Shouts of triumph go up from the men on Hazen's left as they sprint through the cornfield with flags flying and bayonets raised. It's an uphill run as the field begins in a hollow and gradually rises to another wooded ridge. They drive Kelly's outnumbered and exhausted troops to the opposite end of the field, jumping over the dead and wounded who are sprawled in the plowed cornrows. Yelling and panting, they near the end of the field where it disappears into the dark woods. Union sergeant Greg McDermott, running out front, looks up with a glance to see that not only had the "Johnnies stopped and formed," but it appears to him that they've "stopped for good." Rebels, lots of them, are behind a rail fence at the perimeter of the field, pouring rapid fire into Hazen's lines, which are beginning to buckle as the bullets whistle and sing around them. The "Johnnies" McDermott sees behind the fence are those from Baucam's Arkansas regiment who have arrived just in time to shore up the Confederate right.

Up and over the crossbars in the fence, they begin a counterattack, hitting Hazen's bluecoats with a fury. Off to his left, McDermott notices more Rebel fire blasting them from a bluff behind the creek. That punch is coming from the lead elements of Mark Lowery's brigade, streaming onto the high ground above them and pouring fire into the Yankee flank. They are "giving it to us on all sides," growls McDermott. Nearly out of ammunition, Sergeant McDermott and the other survivors are forced back into the corner of the field to form a defensive line along a fence at the wood's edge. "I got back safe enough," recalls McDermott, "until I lay down behind the fence." Once there, a bullet strikes him in the right thigh going "clear through [the] leg." Almost instantly, he notices a boyish looking soldier lying dead beside him, shot in the head and killed "by the same bullet."[19]

Over the past hour, Hazen has sent a steady stream of couriers and staff to the rear urging both Howard and Wood to send him reinforcements. They never respond, and not a soul comes to their aid. The ever-spiteful Nathaniel McLean, supposedly supporting Hazen's right, refuses to move his troops forward. In fact, his only move comes around suppertime when he sends his men into bivouac, claiming they were "entirely without rations." The situation is no better on Hazen's left, where his men have been shot up and run out of the cornfield. Richard Johnson's division has still not arrived. His leading brigade under Ben Scribner has become tangled in the thick bramble on the other side of the creek, and Rebel cavalrymen are picking them off as they try to cross.[20]

Finally, Hazen gives up. Another effort would be futile, and he knows his brigade is beaten. Some of them are still cleaving to the slope of the ridge under Granbury's hostile fire. However, most of them are falling back, and he sees no reason to try to rally them. Some of the survivors, muttering and cursing that they had received no support, gather in a clearing around the gristmill. They all feel as if they've been "sold out." Hazen is there with them when a soldier approaches wanting to know the whereabouts of the general's brigade. Hazen gapes at the man through tears of grief, then in a low voice says, "Brigade, hell, I have none. But what is left is over there in the woods."[21]

Chapter Ten

Tell Mother I Am in the Front Ranks Yet

Gen. Thomas Wood decides to raise the stakes, gambling on the notion that "a second effort might be more successful than the first." Why he hadn't made that effort when Hazen was pleading for reinforcements is unclear. Whatever his reason, he now believes that the odds for another attack stand a better chance of success. After all, the rest of his division has moved forward to a closer jumping-off point and will have a shorter distance to travel than Hazen's brigade. According to Wood, they now have "knowledge of the ground" and know what lies ahead of them. What's more, Wood believes that by this time Richard Johnson is bound to have his troops in position to protect their left flank. Whatever Howard is thinking about making this "second effort" will remain a mystery. If he feels like another catastrophe is being put in motion, he never says so. Maybe he's not euphoric over the idea, but neither does he object. So with Howard's tacit blessing, Wood turns to Col. William Gibson, commander of the brigade immediately behind Hazen's, and orders him to "renew the assault."[1]

At the sound of the bugles, grim-faced Yankee boys from Indiana, Illinois, Ohio, and one bear-hugging regiment from Wisconsin, the descendants of Norwegian Vikings, go tearing off through the woods and into the ravine. Right away Rebel artillery comes alive, filling the air with dirty smoke and deadly missiles. Lt. Alexis Cope, adjutant of the Fifteenth Ohio, watches as his regiment rushes by and fears the attack is doomed to fail. "But there was no diminution in the courage of the men in the ranks," according to Cope, as they dash forward "under a murderous fire of artillery and musketry from a line they could not see." Passing through the ravine and jumping over the crumpled bodies of Hazen's men, the adjutant beholds "a severe cross and enfilading fire from both the enemy's right and left." And just as Hazen's men had discovered during the first charge, the closer they get to the Rebel line of works on the ridge the better off they are from the destructive cannons that are hindered by the angle of their fire. Nevertheless, the rifle fire is treacherous as they begin moving up the slope of the ridge, and Cope recalls how "the minie balls seemed thick as hornets about a nest."[2]

The charge of Gibson's brigade, while following the same general course Hazen had taken, veers off a little farther to the right, some of them spilling out into the small wheat field directly in front of Daniel Govan's Arkansas brigade. Emerging into the clearing, knots of Gibson's men are mowed down in a deadly crossfire unleashed by riflemen from the brigades of both Govan and Granbury. Adding to the mayhem, a Rebel battery that had been placed on Govan's right begins ripping them up with canister. Parrot guns and Howitzers are rocking and bawling in their trenches, spewing jagged metal projectiles across the field and killing or maiming everyone in their sights.

The wounded, becoming more numerous by the minute, continue to fall and carpet the ravine. Their fate is especially perilous. Those who can't crawl away or move behind the safety of a log or tree are pelted over and over by the Rebel shot and shell. "A literal slaughter pen," is how Sgt. Maj. J. A. Gleason describes it in his diary after being caught in the galling crossfire, "rendering it almost useless to seek shelter of rock or tree." Charging from cover to cover, Gleason spots a young soldier petrified with fear and leaning against a tree. Creeping up behind him, he notices that the boy wouldn't lie down even though he wasn't firing his weapon. "In a few minutes a ball came from the left and struck him squarely in the temple, with that particular *spat* which once heard is at once recognized as the passage of a bullet through flesh and bone. It killed him so suddenly that he never changed position" (emphasis added).[3]

Near 6:00 P.M., with Hazen's brigade in shambles and Gibson's troops fully engaged, a courier rushes up to Howard and hands him a message from George Thomas. The note, written at 5:15 P.M., says, in effect, that Sherman has changed his mind, deciding to call off the attack, and wishes for Howard to connect with Schofield in a strong defensive posture. Why Sherman has waited this long to cancel the attack is puzzling, but it may have something to do with his sudden realization that he is facing the entire Confederate Army of Tennessee. That understanding seems to strike him about this same time, and for the first time, he admits it in a note to McPherson headed *sundown.* "No doubt Johnston's whole army is present, as we have felt him for four miles to the north and east." Whatever reason Sherman has for wanting the attack cancelled no longer really matters. The battle is now in full rage.[4]

Down in the ravine, Alexis Cope appeals to a staff officer to go back and find some help to check the blistering crossfire pouring into their flanks. Instead, the officer proposes that Cope himself go to the rear, find Colonel Gibson, and ask for some support. Passing up the slope of the ridge, through the battle-fogged woods, he finally locates Gibson standing with General Wood. "They were both laboring under terrible stress of excitement," remembers Cope, who begins to explain to them the situation at the front. At that moment, Oliver Howard rides up, taking in the adjutant's dismal version of the conditions up ahead. "Go back and tell the men that I will have troops sent in both on their right and left as soon as I can get them," Howard assures him.[5]

Just as Cope begins to start back to his regiment with Howard's promise of reinforcements, a screeching Rebel shell explodes behind him directly over the heads of the three officers. One of the shell fragments strikes Howard in the foot, sending his horse into a wild spin. Reining the startled animal in, Howard cries out, "I am afraid to look down." He hides his eyes behind his empty sleeve, and all he can think about is the horror of another amputation, uttering again, "I am afraid to look down." Turning back, Cope tries to calm him, explaining that the heel of his boot had been blown off, but the foot was still intact. It is, however, black and blue and swelling by the minute. Although "much relieved" to find his foot still attached, Howard is unable to walk or continue riding, and the throbbing pain forces him to the ground where he continues to give orders. Not until the battle is over is he removed to a field hospital.[6]

✳✳✳✳✳✳✳✳✳✳✳✳✳✳

Across the way, on the Union left, Richard Johnson's lead brigade under Ben Scribner is finally in motion. Moving down both sides of the creek, Scribner's troops can hear the rumble of battle erupting from Gibson's charge down in the ravine. Three of Scribner's regiments have crossed over to the east side of the creek only to find themselves swallowed up in briar, bramble, and low-hanging limbs as they make their way up a muddy, wooded ridge. Visibility is so poor here that it's impossible to see the Rebel cavalry skirmishers of Kelly's command, who continue banging away at the columns through the thick foliage. "A volley was fired into us at close range by a line of Rebels who were hidden from our view by a thick growth of small pine trees," writes an Indiana soldier recalling their blind ordeal. Finally, Scribner's men fight their way through the sniping and undergrowth covering the hill and burst into a small wheat field. They march across it, passing the old gristmill where, according to Scribner, they find "the enemy in force, behind their ever-attending breastworks." Here, strong Rebel lines delivering a "galling fire" prevent them from advancing any farther.[7]

West of the creek, on Gibson's immediate left, two more of Scribner's regiments, the Thirty-seventh Indiana and Seventy-eighth Pennsylvania, are still moving forward and coping with the sporadic fire from Rebel sharpshooters. Trotting through the same dark woods that Hazen's left wing had come through earlier, they pass a group of Yankee cavalrymen hunkered down behind a little knoll. "Watch out boys," one of them calls out as they hurry by. The warning is validated as soon as they reach the edge of the infamous cornfield where Hazen's men had been repulsed. Wicked crossfire suddenly fills the air as the two regiments step off into the clearing. "The first man I saw fall was James Little," remembers J. T. Gibson, who moments later has "the misfortune to stop a minie ball of the fifty-nine caliber, which shattered the bone of my left arm and lodged in my shoulder." Gibson assumes that Private Little was "instantly killed," but when Chaplain Richard Christy reaches him the youngster is still alive. Little breathes his last words in the arms of the Catholic priest: "Tell mother I am in the front ranks yet."[8]

As they begin moving across the open field, Scribner's men are becoming desperate for cover as Rebel fire begins pelting them.

"Our men picked up rails, old chunks and logs for breastworks and laid down behind them," recollects Sergeant Puntenny. One of the first men to grab a log is Indiana private J. J. Kirk, who is criticized by the man beside him for what he considers to be a futile precaution. Kirk retorts, "You will be glad to get your head behind this log before long." The answer proves prophetic, as minutes later both men are taking cover behind that same log while the bullets are "flying thick" in a withering fire. "You made fun of me for carrying this log, and just as I said you are the first man to get behind it." Before his friend can answer, a ball passes through the rotten log hitting Kirk in the head. Although his face is a bloody mess, Kirk is alive, as the bullet, moving through the log, lost the momentum necessary to kill him.[9]

Scribner's troops have been issued the standard sixty rounds of ammunition, and it's beginning to look as if they'll need every last one of them. Across the way, through the cornfield, they can see the clusters of butternut and gray soldiers swarming between the swirls of yellow smoke. There's hardly any order to the Rebel formation, but according to J. T. Gibson, "they seemed to be countless in numbers" and moving toward them in a counterattack like an angry mob. The awful outcry of the Rebel Yell rings out from their ranks as they trot closer and closer. The two blue regiments are battered with intense fire, and the numbers of killed and wounded begin to mount as they stagger from the lines or sprawl to the ground. Still, they manage to hold their ground. "They fired their last cartridge and then took from their dead comrades the cartridges they had," writes Sergeant Puntenny, reminiscing his regiment's gallant stand.[10]

As the number of Confederates continues to increase, it's obvious that Cleburne has been reinforced. Lowery's and Kelly's troops have been joined by William Quarles's brigade, which had traveled by rail from Mobile to Marietta, arriving only last night. They are veteran infantrymen from Louisiana and Tennessee, and Hood had ordered them to double-time to the army's right flank in support of Cleburne. Later, the Irishman will remark that they were "providentially sent." Now with the field crowded with Rebels of several commands, the Union left flank is threatened. Jumpy officers from Scribner's brigade are worried, fearing that the situation is becoming futile. Richard Johnson, the division commander, has already been carried from the field, struck in the hip by an unexploded cannon ball. Scribner is in the rear with the rest of his brigade and either won't or can't react. At least three times, word is sent back to him to send help and ammunition. But Scribner never responds. Afterward, some of his men will complain that he was drunk. Others, like Sergeant Puntenny, are a bit more discreet in their criticism: "The reason no aid was sent is not creditable to the Brigade Commander, and I will say nothing about it." With their ammunition nearly exhausted, Scribner's troops have no choice but to fall back, as the Confederates continue to mass on their front and left.[11]

****

Back on the right, Gibson's brigade has passed through the bloody ravine, and the survivors are clawing their way up the ridge. They are suffering the identical fate as Hazen's troops. Only this time it's worse. In fact, by the time they reach the narrow killing ground below the crest of the ridge, their losses are even greater than Hazen's, who admits that his brigade suffered "its first and only unsuccessful effort during the war." Still without any support on their flanks, Gibson's lines continue to charge headlong into a steady stream of lead poured out from the Confederate brigades of Granbury and Govan. Determined, they press on, and in places, the blue and gray lines actually brush against each other, igniting into a flurry of rage. "The fact is," claims Arkansas veteran Stan Harley, "it was about three or four hours of the closest fighting in which we were ever caught, and that is saying a good deal." Pvt. George Tabor, one of Granbury's men, who is wounded twice before sundown, agrees that the fracas was "as near a hand-to-hand fight as I ever participated in during the war."[12]

Finally, Gibson's brigade begins to break apart, and his troops stagger down the ridge back into the ravine and the sights of the Rebel cannoneers blasting away at them as they retreat. By now, it's 6:30 P.M. The sky is growing darker with each passing minute, and the pious Oliver Howard is satisfied that the Lord is not going to grant him a victory. Understanding this, and in keeping with

Sherman's orders to cancel the attack, Howard hurries to bring to an end what he can only call "a sort of nightmare."[13] He orders Wood to send in his last remaining brigade, which is commanded by Col. Frederick Knefler, to cover Gibson's retreat, recover as many wounded as possible, and set up a defensive line. In attempting this, Knefler funnels his brigade into the ravine, where they run into Gibson's fleeing soldiers, resulting in a jumble of men exposed to the murderous Rebel crossfire. Fading light is all that saves them from the destructive shot and shell of the Rebel gunners, whose targets are soon lost in the shadowy terrain. Until it is totally dark, Knefler's men work to remove the wounded, but many remain in the ravine. Of those left behind, some aren't wounded at all, but are simply afraid to move, choosing to remain under the cover of a log or tree. Finally, Knefler manages to organize a line of defense strung out in the woods beyond the ravine where they are joined by the survivors of Scribner's two battered regiments and some stragglers from Hazen's and Gibson's brigades. There, from behind hastily thrown-up breastworks, they trade shots with the Rebels across the way until the shooting dwindles to a sputter.[14]

In the rear, Union surgeons have set up a field hospital, where a continuous flow of wounded await treatment. Howard is among them, his foot throbbing with pain from the shrapnel bruise he had received earlier. "I sat that night among the wounded in the midst of a forest glade," he writes later when remembering the awful aftermath. Grieving over the wounding of General Johnson and Captain Stinson of his own staff, who had been shot through both lungs, Howard watches the suffering of countless others, recalling that "a large number lay there, on a sideling slope by a faint camp-fire, with broken limbs and disfigured faces."[15]

Chapter Eleven

The Most Trying Time

The blackness of night settles over the woods, shrouding the carnage of the awful battle. Down in the ravine, gun smoke hangs in the still air, and a misting rain is beginning to fall from low, murky clouds, veiling the moon and stars. The only light at all comes from the steady glow of some burning pine trees, fat with resin, splintered and set afire during the Rebel cannonade. Elsewhere, nothing can be seen across the forest floor except the occasional flashes of gunfire winking through the ravine. Between the sporadic cracks of those rifles, the landscape is quiet. "So still," according to Confederate captain Sam Foster, "that the chirp of a cricket could be heard 100 feet away." But the silence is deceiving. Many Union soldiers, mostly from Knefler's brigade and some survivors of the vicious attacks launched by Hazen and Gibson, are dangerously close to the gray lines. From his position, Foster judges a number of them to be "not more than 40 feet in front of us." Cocking his ear, he can hear the Federal soldiers moving through the leaves and underbrush, collecting their dead and wounded "like hogs rooting for acorns, but not speaking a word above a whisper."[1]

Like Captain Foster, Pat Cleburne can also hear the footsteps of Yankee soldiers, calculating them to be "in great numbers immediately in front of portions of my lines." Concerned that the enemy has not completely withdrawn, Cleburne tells Hiram Granbury and Mark Lowery to send out skirmishers and "learn the state of things in their respective fronts." Granbury, believing this would be "impossible" with the enemy in such close proximity, instead proposes that he advance with his whole brigade. Cleburne has never been one to attempt a night attack unless ordered to do so. There are simply too many risks involved

117

in fighting at night over unknown ground, and those risks are especially dangerous here at Pickett's Mill in such a junglelike terrain. Ordinarily Cleburne would have refused Granbury's plan as reckless, but here, in this situation, he apparently considers it necessary and grants his approval.[2]

Around 10:00 P.M., a bugle blares splitting the dark stillness and signaling Granbury's Texans to charge the enemy. "We raised a regular Texas Yell, or an Indian Yell or perhaps both together," remembers Foster. Then they lunge forward, running downhill into the ravine "still yelling like all the devils from the lower regions had been turned loose." And across the ravine, Union colonel Ben Scribner, who has already been accused of being drunk, listens in a sobering realization as the Rebels "came rushing and shouting like demons." Hearing the screams of so many Confederate soldiers drawing closer, panicky Union soldiers have little doubt as to what is happening. "Now the Rebels are coming," a Wisconsin soldier says solicitously to his friend Hans Gunderson standing beside him. "Yes," replies Gunderson, "then I'm sure as hell not going to stay here any longer, and he went off into the dark." Gunderson is only one of many who flee after hearing the first wails of the approaching Rebels. So it seems that Sam Foster is correct when he writes in his diary, "The noise we made with our mouths was too much for them."[3]

But the charge is not limited to the angry clamor of a thousand yelping throats. "We commenced to fire as soon as we started," says Foster, and instantly "the Yanks turned loose," shooting uphill at the charging Texans. Running down the rocky slope, Granbury's men struggle to maintain their sense of direction. "We could not see anything at all," complains Captain Foster, recalling their blind stumble through the dark thickets covering the hill. As the fire grows heavier, "the flash of their guns would light up the woods like a flash of lightning," and the Rebels are able to catch glimpses of shadowy figures moving below in their front. Some of them whirl and break for the rear while many simply throw up their hands and sink to their knees. "All they could say was 'don't shoot, don't shoot!'" recalls Foster. Others fight back as the floor of the ravine becomes crowded with clusters of cursing men, fighting hand to hand, and going at each other with gun butts and bayonets.[4]

Foster later remarks, "To make that charge in the dark was the most trying time I experienced during the whole war." Trying though it was, the charge is successful, and Granbury's men, like a pack of hyenas, continue to drive headlong into the startled Union soldiers, creating a scene of panic and confusion. By now, most of the Federals have begun to break for what they perceive to be the rear. Unfortunately, no one seems exactly sure which way they should go, and bluecoats are running and staggering off in every direction through the forbidding woods. For example, Pvt. Sivert Lee decides that he will be better off to leave the cover of his log and, as he puts it, "leg it" to the rear. Tearing through the black brush, he loses his balance, and sprawls to the ground, dropping his rifle in the process. "I was alone," complains Lee of his ordeal, "I went in what I thought was the right direction and stopped for a moment by a tree to get my bearings, and then I was surrounded by boys in gray, and now no prayer could help. I just had to go with them."[5]

Lee, of course, is not the only Union soldier forced to go with the boys in gray. So taken by surprise at the sudden attack, many of them simply freeze in place and are easily captured. "We kept finding them as we advanced," says Sam Foster, "and occasionally a tree lying on the ground would have from 5 to 20 Yanks lying down behind the log." These are herded to the rear, and Granbury's Texans keep prowling forward into the inky ravine, chasing the fleeing Federals toward their main line of defense, and collecting floundering prisoners along the way. Before the night is over, 232 Union men will be captured and on their way to the infamous Andersonville prison. Routing the enemy and bagging so many prisoners delights Cleburne, who compliments Granbury and his Texans for "the brilliancy of this night attack," which he feels only added "luster" to what they had already accomplished this day.[6]

The attack finally ends when some of the Texans begin encountering stiff resistance from the Yankee skirmish lines and can no longer safely pursue the enemy. Others, like Foster, could chase them no farther, becoming confused and disoriented in the turmoil of the dark forest. "We lost trail of the enemy and our men were badly mixed up," admits Foster.[7] Some of them have become hopelessly lost and are growing desperate trying to find their way back. Such is the mood of young Lt. Thomie Stokes, who finds the Confederate lines after getting lost, then describes the anxious ordeal in a letter to his sister:

Here I was, alone in the darkness of midnight, with the wounded, the dying, and the dead. What an hour of horror! I hope never again to experience such. I am not superstitious, but the great excitement of seven hours of fierce conflict, ending with a bold, and I might say reckless charge—for we knew not what was in our front—and then left entirely alone, causes a mental and physical depression that for one to fully appreciate he must be surrounded by the same circumstances. My feelings in battle were nothing to compare to this hour. After going first one way and then another, and not bettering my case, I heard someone slipping along in the bushes. I commanded him to halt, and inquired what regiment he belonged to, and was answered, "15th Wisconsin" so I took Mr. Wisconsin in, and ordered him to march before me—a nice pickle for me then, had a prisoner and did not know where to go. Moved on, however, and finally heard some men walking, hailed them, for I had become desperate, and was answered "Mississippians." Oh how glad I was.[8]

****

This same night while Granbury's men are finding their way back to Cleburne's lines, a stirring of some magnitude is taking place behind them. Thousands of soldiers from Hood's corps are quietly slipping out of their ditches, forming into columns, and marching off into the darkness in a northeastward direction. This night march begins another aggressive scheme concocted by John Bell Hood. This time he plans to sneak around the Federal left and strike the enemy at first light while they are still in a state of confusion after being repulsed by Cleburne. From Wheeler's cavalry Hood has learned that the extreme left of Sherman's army is beyond Pickett's Mill Creek, separated from the main body and vulnerable to flank attack. "Encouraged by this favorable opportunity of dealing the enemy a hard blow," Hood remembers, "I instantly repaired to General Johnston's headquarters and asked his permission to withdraw my corps at dark from our extreme right, and attack this exposed flank next morning." Johnston, though somewhat reluctant to bring on a "general engagement," consents to the plan, and according to Hood, tells Hardee and

Polk "to hold their corps in readiness for action the next day" to assist him in case a full-blown battle should ensue. At the same time, Polk is ordered to shift his corps to the right, occupying the ground vacated by Hood.[9]

Hood, now as always, seems ready to exploit any opportunity to attack. He had come to Johnston and the Army of Tennessee advertised as a man who likes to fight and a student of the Lee and Jackson school of warfare. Even though Johnston has never subscribed to the audacious tactics of those generals and is regarded by some as an overly cautious commander, he has a high opinion of the pugnacious Hood. Not only has Johnston welcomed him to the army, he's also sought his counsel and advice above that of his more experienced corps commanders, Polk and Hardee. Johnston's acceptance of Hood's plan for a flank attack here in the woods surrounding the Pickett settlement is further evidence of his faith in the Kentuckian's abilities. It's also apparent that Johnston is not yet aware of Hood's self-serving correspondence to Davis, Bragg, and the authorities in Richmond wherein he has repeatedly portrayed his commander as weak and lacking the offensive qualities necessary to lead an army and, at the same time, hinting that he could do a better job. Hood, it seems, is extremely ambitious, and his motive for trying to discredit Johnston is clear. His desire to command the Army of Tennessee has driven him to create a false impression with the government regarding Johnston and the situation in North Georgia. Throughout the campaign, he has told them that Johnston had not and would not consider any offensive tactic, even though he has continually urged him to do so. While this isn't exactly true, it leaves both Davis and Bragg wondering if Hood could be the man that might remedy their troubles in Georgia.[10]

Hood's idea of dealing with Sherman and saving Atlanta is simple: Attack. The full-blown charge seems to be the only tactic Hood has ever learned. He may be short an arm and leg, but he isn't the type to sit behind breastworks and wait on the enemy. No, not Hood, not as long as he has another limb or so left to lose. He prefers the offensive, and even the suggestion of fighting behind breastworks irks him. In his opinion, too much entrenching "renders troops timid in battle." And pitched battle is just the venue Hood believes a Southern soldier should be, where he's "taught to rely solely upon his own valor." Everyone should come on out from behind those breastworks, fight like men, and "charge into the cauldron, wherever it is, whatever it is." Ironically, this kind of warfare, preferred by Hood, is exactly what has rendered him sling-armed and left him with a nub for a leg. "Look what they done to old Hood!" his Texans had wailed after seeing him fall at Chickamauga. The fallacies of his naïve approach to war in the face of an enemy with superior numbers should have become apparent to Hood by this time. Even now, here in the Hell Hole, Confederate forces have achieved two quick victories, fighting from hastily prepared defensive positions. And whether he knows it or not, Robert E. Lee, whom he has long admired for his open-field charges and bold flanking movements, has taken up the spade and started fighting from ditches back in Virginia. Yet Hood will continue to embrace the frontal attack and scorn the idea of entrenching.[11]

✻✻✻✻✻✻✻✻✻✻✻✻✻✻

So now comes John Bell Hood strapped in his saddle, flanked by cavalry guides, and leading his corps through the forest on a blind night march to what he hopes will be a surprise attack on Sherman's left flank. By midnight, the long gray columns are all in motion, slowly feeling their way through the tangled, black woods and snaking along toward the end of the Federal line. The march is a long and strenuous one, taking them through six or seven miles of rough and broken country. Since there are so many men struggling to get through such a wild and twisted terrain, there are constant stops and delays along the way.

Among Hood's many soldiers is Pvt. Hiram Smith Williams, tottering along in one of the columns with no idea of where they're going or what it is they'll do when they get there. Just another private following the private in front of him, he only knows that the journey is difficult and says so: "Along the crookedest [sic] roads to be found, across streams, up hills, down in ravines, we pursued our weary way." They march all night, and in the first gray streaks of dawn, the lines of sleepy worn-out men are brought to a halt. Wheeler's scouts have stopped Hood, telling him that he had just as well turn around and go back. The Yankees, it seems, have crossed the creek at Pickett's Mill and thrown up fortifications. All through the night, they say they've listened to the sounds of the enemy "cutting down trees" and building their works. Hood hears them out, scribbles a note to Johnston advising him of this new development, and sends it by one of his aides.[12]

It's midmorning before Hood's aide reaches Johnston. He finds him at Cleburne's headquarters pacing the ground and patiently waiting for "the sounds of Hood's musketry." After reading Hood's message, Johnston can only agree with his corps commander's assessment that to attack now would be "folly" and admits "that there could be no surprise, which was necessary to success." But for the warrior Hood to suggest that an attack should not be made, in spite of adverse conditions, such as the loss of surprise and the presence of formidable breastworks, seems out of character. Oddly, this is not the first attack he has advised against making since the campaign began. So has Hood merely shown some rare prudence here in advising against the attack, or is this just another deliberate attempt to convince the government in Richmond that Johnston refuses to take the tactical offensive? Whatever the case, Johnston, with little choice, orders Hood and Polk to return to their former positions.[13]

Thus ends what Pvt. Williams describes in his diary entry of May 28 as "one of the strangest movements of the whole campaign." In his mind, the march, when completed, resembled a huge "figure 8" landing them right back at the same spot they had started. But after tramping out the long, circuitous procession, Williams is too tired to care. "I am very weary," he moans as he returns to the same familiar ditch he had come from the night before.[14]

Chapter Twelve

A Great Blue Carpet

May 28, 1864, breaks into another humid and sultry day. When there's light enough to see, Confederate soldiers around the Pickett Settlement can now behold the ugly remains of the once virgin forest. The trees have been splintered and ripped apart, tops blown out, some of them still smoldering from the fire of artillery. Below the canopy of trees, the undergrowth is trampled, bushes stomped down, scrub oaks twisted, bent, and scarred by grape shot and canister. Like after any battle, debris litters the landscape. The forest floor is covered in torn paper cartridges that dot the ground along with discarded equipment of every description: Knapsacks, canteens, bedrolls, ammo boxes, weapons, straps, belts, and pieces of uniform, all forsaken, cast aside, and scattered in the leaves as tokens of the savage fight. Added to the many signs of ruin is the Widow Pickett's gristmill, which at some point in the fray has burned to its foundation.[1]

But the real wreckage is human and causes soldiers to shudder as they try to comprehend the carnage. "Such a scene," writes Thomie Stokes in a letter to his sister. "Here lay the wounded, the dying, and the dead, hundreds upon hundreds, in every conceivable position; some with contorted features, showing the agony of death, others as if quietly sleeping. . . . Though they had been my enemies, my heart bled at the sickening scene." For William Oliphant, the ravine looked as if "a great blue carpet had been spread over the ground. Dead men were everywhere. They lay in solid lines just as they fell, and in many places they lay in heaps." And a Mississippi witness, Columbus Sykes, seems to agree with Oliphant's metaphor, "a great blue carpet," when he writes in a letter to his wife, "They were lying piled so thick that I could, had I chosen, walked over a large portion of the field on their mutilated bodies."[2]

Throughout this sweltering Saturday, other Rebel soldiers, who had listened from their distant positions to the rumble of yesterday's battle and wondered what it meant, have continued to come and view the spectacle. Bromfield Ridley and A. P. Stewart's son, Caruthers, are among them, having wandered onto the battlefield from the ditches in front of New Hope Church. Ridley, writing years later in his journal, recalls "the seething mass of quivering flesh, the dead piled upon each other and the groans of the dying." The scene was repulsive, but one memory is especially disturbing and continues to haunt him through the years. "I have so often thought of two little boys that we saw among the dead Federals. They appeared to be about fourteen years old, and were exactly alike. Their hands were clasped in death." Ridley assumes "the little boys must have been twin brothers."[3]

According to the account of Pvt. William Oliphant, several generals, including the corps commanders Hardee, Hood, and Polk "came and viewed the ground." Even Joe Johnston joins the parade of spectators "gazing intently upon the scene." By this time, stretcher-bearers are gathering the wounded while gravediggers begin opening mass, shallow graves into which the bloodstained dead are randomly tossed and covered up. Unfortunately, some of these will soon be exposed by the wash of torrential rains, or perhaps rooted back up by feral hogs within a matter of days. Watching the ghoulish burials, the onlookers can't help but notice that the ratio of dead to wounded is higher than anything they've seen in the past. This anomaly occurs only because the wounded men, who could not move or be moved, were shot repeatedly where they fell. Some of the Yankee corpses are riddled with bullets from the continuous exposure, and in one of them alone, Rebel soldiers count forty-seven bullet holes.[4]

As always, after any Rebel victory, the usual plundering is underway. Ragged Confederates are prowling among the corpses, relieving them of anything they find of value, including clothing, shoes, guns, food, and personal items. Capt. Sam Foster is no exception, taking all the contents from a Yankee's knapsack; "all of which except the knapsack, I appropriate for my own use. I also find scattered here and there tin cups, tin plates—haversacks with knife & fork, bacon and crackers, coffee, *surenough coffee*. Oh I am rich; crackers, bacon & coffee." In addition to that booty, he finds guns "with plenty of ammunition." But Foster, who counts fifty dead men within the thirty-foot radius where he stands, is eager to leave the battlefield, writing in his diary, "Here I beheld that which I cannot describe and hope never to see again."[5]

Word of the Confederate victory soon spreads across Georgia, bringing new hope to its citizens that Sherman might soon be forced to abandon his campaign and turn back. "Glorious news from the front," crows the *Augusta Chronicle & Sentinel*, "General Cleburne ambuscades the enemy. Between five and six thousand Yankees killed." By exaggerating the number of killed, the paper may have achieved the desired effect of thrilling its anxious readers, but the assertion is no less absurd. Although it was clearly a one-sided victory for Johnston's army, Federal casualties are much lower than what the Augusta paper has represented. In fact, total losses, including killed, wounded, and captured, are calculated to be 1,732, of which nearly 85 percent were listed in Thomas Wood's division. The Confederates, on the other hand, have inflicted nearly four times the damage they've suffered, as Cleburne only reports a total of 448 casualties of all categories.[6]

* * * * * * * * * * * * * *

Although Sherman has no intention of turning back, he does admit in a telegram to Henry Halleck and the War Department in Washington that "Johnston has chosen a strong line, and made hasty but strong parapets of timber and earth, and has thus far stopped us." What he does not admit is that since stumbling into the Hell Hole his army has suffered defeats on May 25 and 27, only conceding, "We have had many sharp, severe encounters, but nothing decisive." Since neither army has been forced from its original position, Sherman is correct in claiming that such encounters were "nothing decisive." However, two of those encounters were not only "sharp" and "severe," but were clearly defeats for Sherman—a fact not lost on the Union soldiers who had taken part in them. So far, his army has incurred nearly 3,500 casualties in two pitched battles and hundreds more in the constant skirmishing taking place along the eight-mile front between Pickett's Mill and Dallas.[7]

By now, May 28, Sherman sees that his latest grand flanking

movement is not achieving the hoped-for results. Even though Johnston has been forced to vacate his strong position in the Allatoona Mountains, he has not been driven to or across the Chattahoochee but has instead pulled Sherman into a bloody stalemate in the Georgia wilderness, miles from his vital railroad supply line. And for the first time, Sherman realizes the difficulties of maintaining his huge army for any length of time without that vital artery. Since crossing the Etowah River at Kingston, his troops have not enjoyed full rations, and the animals are beginning to suffer from lack of forage. Previously abundant supplies are now scarce because the wagons from Kingston are continually bogged down and delayed on the narrow, muddy roads, which are not much more than pig trails winding through the thickets. After four days of meager sustenance, grumbling soldiers are cinching up their belts while half-ton horses and mules resort to eating plants and bushes and even chewing the bark off trees.[8]

Thus Sherman, finding himself in what he sardonically describes as "a state of nature—with few or no roads, nothing that a European could understand" (but a predicament he can surely appreciate), resolves to return to his lifeline. He makes his intentions known in a telegram to General Halleck: "I am gradually working round by the left to approach the railroad." Before this can happen, however, Sherman must unite James McPherson's command at Dallas with the rest of the army, closing the gap between that general and George Thomas's right wing. About midmorning on Saturday, May 28, McPherson receives Sherman's order to begin moving to his left and connect with Thomas's right. Attempting this move will be dangerous, and McPherson knows it. If the Confederates were to detect such a shift, they would surely take action to prevent it, attacking his exposed columns. So McPherson decides to wait for nightfall, ordering his troops to begin pulling out of their breastworks under the cover of darkness.[9]

* * * * * * * * * * * * * *

This same morning finds Joe Johnston still searching for an opportunity to make a bold offensive move. But *bold* is hardly the adjective to describe the reserved and cautious soldier from Virginia. Psychologically, offensive warfare is against everything in his nature, and he's just witnessed the suicidal results of attacking prepared breastworks here in the Hell Hole, which adds to his wariness. To this point in the campaign, he realizes that he's done very little to inspire confidence with Davis and Bragg that he can drive Sherman out of Georgia. It seems that every time he anticipates an offensive movement something goes wrong. "Events beyond my control having prevented my attacking the enemy," he complains. Only this morning, Hood's attempt to attack the Federal left had to be aborted in the face of newly constructed breastworks and the loss of surprise. It was another failed opportunity, another disappointment, and maybe for the first time, Johnston is beginning to question Hood's advice and abilities as a commander, although he's still not aware of his disloyalty. Nevertheless, the results are still his responsibility, and he's becoming disheartened and frustrated at his inability to take the offensive. In part, he blames this on Sherman's style of warfare, which is cautious, methodical, and siegelike, with huge flanking movements compelling him to retreat constantly. The same complaint so often heard by Sherman when referring to the wily Johnston is now being echoed by Johnston about Sherman when he grumbles, "I can find no opportunity to attack him except behind intrenchments."[10]

Johnston's pessimism, however, is at least tempered by the fact that he's intercepted Sherman here in the Hell Hole, where he has spoiled his latest flanking movement, achieved two defensive victories, and still has him pinned down miles from his rail supply. Under the circumstances, Johnston believes that this was the best he could do. Although he's yet to attack Sherman, he interprets the results of his defensive strategy for the past several days as a success and says so in a telegram to Richmond, which he sends to Bragg this same day. "We are still confronting the enemy here," he assures him, then goes on to briefly describe his defensive victories, "Hooker's corps . . . repulsed with considerable loss" and "Howard's corps . . . defeated with slaughter."[11] Since Johnston rarely shares any news of the front with Davis or Bragg, the point of this wire is clearly to convince them of the success in his defensive strategy and the somewhat bizarre notion that he can win by not losing.

But now Johnston believes he may have another chance to take the offensive against Sherman. Even though Hood's attack on the Federal left had to be canceled, there may be another opportunity to strike their right. Cavalry scouts from Red Jackson's division have been bringing him reports that McPherson's troops are moving to the northeast, pulling back. What the scouts are seeing from their position atop Elsberry Mountain, however, are probably only preparations for the movement McPherson plans to make after nightfall. Whatever the case, the false reports encourage Johnston to at least explore the chance of catching the Federals outside their breastworks and launch an attack. Johnston is also aware of the gap separating McPherson and Thomas and may suspect the movement as an attempt to link their forces. Accordingly, he decides to probe the Federal right and orders General Hardee to send the division of William B. Bate, now occupying the extreme left of the Confederate line, to make a reconnaissance in force. So Hardee sends word to Bate, "General Johnston desires you to develop the enemy, ascertain his strength and position, as it is believed he is not in force." If Johnston's postulation proves to be true, then Bate is to go ahead and attack the enemy works and push ahead and occupy the town of Dallas.[12]

Attacking the Federal right is an assignment that suits William Bate. "Fighting Billy," as some call him, is a soldier who will lead a charge anywhere, do anything, and has a burning itch for glory. Others have given him the less flattering but more popular nickname "Old Grits" and have little love for a man they consider an insensitive, almost draconian disciplinarian. The thirty-seven-year-old Bate has no formal education, military or otherwise, but had studied law and edited a newspaper before the war and somewhere along the way developed a massive ego. He's an odd-looking man, dark complected, a blade for a nose, full curly beard, and speaks with a high-pitched, squeaky voice. His soldiers know he's not a man to be trifled with, and they snap to attention when he passes. They remember the battle at Shiloh, when a bullet tore through his leg as he led a valiant charge. That same bullet killed his horse, a stallion named Black Hawk, and that noble animal was only one of six shot from under him during the war. Later, when the surgeons attempted to amputate the leg, Grits produced a pistol and leveled it on the doctors, announcing his intention to

William B. Bate (Prints and Photographs Division, Library of Congress)

"protect that leg." He did just that. Now, two years later, Bate is hobbling through the woods of North Georgia with a permanent limp, but the shot-up leg is still with him.[13]

After receiving Hardee's directive, Bate sends a written order to his brigade commanders, and then calls them together in an "interview," making sure they understand his instructions. More convinced than Johnston, Bate is satisfied that McPherson has already moved most of his troops out of their fortifications. "In my own mind," he shrills, "the enemy is not in force nor heavily entrenched on my front." But in keeping with Johnston's orders, he adds the caveat that upon "coming in contact with stubborn resistance behind defenses," they should "withdraw without assault unless satisfied it can be carried." Then, throwing caution to the wind, Bate goes on to explain his plan of attack. Frank Armstrong's brigade of dismounted cavalry from Jackson's division will go in first, hitting the Federal far right. The signal for them to advance will be a single volley from Maj. Robert Cobb's battery. Once Armstrong's movement is executed and the "opposition ceases," the three infantry brigades will advance on the signal of two volleys from Cobb's battery. Advancing from left to right, Thomas Smith's brigade of Tennesseans will move first; followed by Finley's Florida brigade, presently commanded by Robert Bullock; and finally Joe Lewis's Kentuckians. However, if Armstrong should happen to find the Yankees there in force, stacked up behind breastworks, then the second signal will not be given, and the infantry brigades will not move. Thus, "the whole advance movement of the infantry," Bate stresses, "depends on the result of General Jackson's [Armstrong's] cavalry."[14]

By midafternoon, Frank Armstrong's troops are filing into the ditches vacated by Bate's infantrymen, who have moved a few hundred yards to the north in preparation for the attack. For the most part, they are doughty Mississippians—hard, filthy men dressed in grimy gray and faded butternut—who before being transferred here had ridden with the living legend, Nathan Bedford Forrest. Forrest, of course, is nowhere near this Georgia battlefield, a fact that pleases Sherman, who has continued to worry throughout the campaign that "that devil" might suddenly show up behind him, rampaging over his lines of supply and communications, and wreaking his usual havoc. But with Forrest preoccupied miles away back in Mississippi, Sherman will only have to contend with Armstrong's troops, who have grown mean and tough under the "Wizard's" tutelage. They are veterans of many battles and have earned a reputation as bold fighters. Ordinarily, cavalrymen are not held in high esteem by the infantry, mostly because of their shyness about fighting on foot. But Armstrong's Mississippians seem to be the exception. They have no problem dismounting and playing the role of infantrymen, and by this stage of the war, they are quite inured to that part. Even Forrest, who is stingy with a compliment and rarely impressed with mortal man, agrees; "Armstrong's brigade while fighting on foot would be credible to the best drilled infantry."[15]

There's a deadly stretch of boredom while Armstrong's Mississippians wait in the ditches for the signal to attack. Having nothing to do but listen to the monotonous clatter of sniper fire, Frank Montgomery, lieutenant colonel of the First Mississippi, decides to get a better look at the Yankee breastworks his men will soon be ordered to attack. Their lines are only two hundred yards apart, but the woods are thick, making it necessary for Montgomery to gain a better vantage point for observation. "I walked carefully along the works to a battery on a hill just a little ways off," he remembers. After climbing the hill, "I stopped a moment to look through an embrasure at the battery, and a half-dozen minnie-balls hissed viciously by my head, and I quickly got behind the fortifications. I caught, however, a good look at part of their works, which seemed very strong and were well manned." Alarmed by the sight, Montgomery tells his regimental commander, Col. R. A. Pinson, what he has seen, "and that I was satisfied that the enemy were in their works in force." But Pinson tells him the attack will proceed as planned. Bate has already assured Armstrong that the fortifications have been weakened and only defended by a skirmish line. Bate, it seems, is confident that the attack here at Dallas will be successful, resulting in what he hopes will be another "great blue carpet," just like the Confederates had accomplished at Pickett's Mill. Montgomery disagrees but is "powerless" to argue and resigns himself to the fact that there's "nothing to do but obey."[16]

Chapter Thirteen

We Knew We Had Met
Them in Vain

Atop a rise looking west, Confederate soldiers of the First
Tennessee regiment watch from their reserve position as
Armstrong's dismounted cavalrymen spring from their ditches
and draw up in line of battle. Among the onlookers is Pvt. Sam
Watkins, who is enamored at the sight of Frank Armstrong,
describing him as "grand and glorious" as he rides to the center
of the column. Watkins hears the general address his men in
a voice booming with charm and authority: "Soldiers, we have
been selected to go forward and capture yon heights. Do you
think we can take them? I will lead the attack." Watkins listens as
"the men whooped, and the cry, 'we can, we can' was heard from
one end of the line to the other." Above the cheers and shouts a
single cannon shot rings out at 3:45 P.M., signaling the attack to
begin. Officers can be heard calling out the order, "Forward, guide
center, march!" They disappear into the woods, moving down a
little ravine, and then emerge into an open field where Watkins
sees them again, inspiring him to describe it as "the grandest
spectacle I ever witnessed."[1]

Beyond that field, on the Federal far right, the soldiers of
William Harrow's division of the XV Corps are tucked in their
breastworks and directly in the path of the coming storm. They
are Midwesterners, Illinois men for the most part, who are killing
time on what seems to be a peaceful enough afternoon. Boiling
coffee and playing cards, the men have learned to ignore the
constant patter of sniper fire and random skirmishing, which is
always with them. But suddenly the routine of their day is abruptly
broken when the ground in front of them comes alive in a distant
chorus of shrieks and yells. Startled by the uproar, Capt. Charles
Wills, 103rd Illinois, peers over a head log toward the source of

the commotion and sees "a heavy column of Rebels" bursting out of the woods "with a yell the devil ought to copyright."[2]

Harrow's troops scramble for their weapons and a position from which they can fire them. Instantly the clatter of their guns begins to be heard by soldiers farther up the Union lines where the divisions of Morgan Smith and Peter Osterhaus are entrenched on the slope of a spinelike ridge near the Villa Rica Road that runs north to the town of Dallas. Just as the men of Harrow's division were surprised by the sudden attack, so too were Morgan Smith's troops whose position is on Harrow's immediate left. In fact, Smith and his staff are enjoying a quiet nap when the roar of gunfire rolls them from their slumber and sends them running for their horses. One member of Smith's staff, Maj. Thomas Taylor, a lawyer from Ohio before the war, is shocked by the unexpected assault, and recalls the moment when he and the others galloped off in the direction of the firing. "Hardly had we reached the road," he writes to his wife, Netta, "when a most terrific storm broke over our lines and came rolling toward us—demonic yells were the interludes. The enemy was charging—assaulting our works."[3]

Across the way, Armstrong's Rebel brigade never pauses; shooting and whooping it up, they quickly overrun the blue skirmish lines. Charging in columns of regiments, they quickly surround and capture a battery of three cannons of the First Iowa, which had been moved to a forward position beyond the Union earthworks. Sam Watkins and his fellow Tennesseans continue to watch attentively from the distant rise behind the little ravine. "We could see the smoke and dust of battle, and hear the shout of the charge, and the roar and rattle of cannon and musketry." And they also see that Frank Armstrong is paying a terrible price for the ground his troops are taking as Watkins continues to recount the spectacle before him. "We can see the line of dead and wounded along the tracks over which he passed, and finally we see our battle-flag planted upon the Federal breastworks. I cannot describe the scene."[4]

The scene, however grand Sam Watkins may see it, is short lived. John "Black Jack" Logan, the flamboyant and capable commander of the XV Corps, is now taking quick and decisive action to drive the Rebels back. Logan, one of Sherman's few political generals, counterpunches with a brigade he orders down from Peter Osterhaus's division; "arriving just in time to assist our comrades," declares the German-born Osterhaus, who personally leads the brigade into action. Logan is also in the midst of the fray, riding among his troops and shouting words of encouragement. Waving his hat, his black hair flowing and dark eyes gleaming, the general calls out, "Give them hell boys." And Captain Wills remembers being heartened when Logan stops his horse beside the young officer and says, "It's all right, damn it, isn't it?" Satisfied when Wills calls back, "It's all right General," Logan keeps right on moving through the knots of fighting men and the battle, which he describes as "close and deadly."[5]

As the fight continues to swell, Col. John Wilder's "Lightning Brigade" of mounted infantry armed with their deadly repeating Spencer carbines also comes to the support of Logan, guarding his refused right flank. Although the Rebels manage to penetrate a breach in the Union earthworks, they soon find themselves not only outnumbered, but completely outgunned as Wilder's men are rapidly clipping off seven shots while Armstrong's troops methodically swab their rifle barrels in the old Napoleonic fashion. "Line after line was sent back broken," claims Logan, recalling the failed Rebel charge, which he calculates was over in half an hour.[6]

Armstrong's assault is a bloody failure; its sole success is the discovery that the Union fortifications are strong after all, and any attempt to break them would be futile. This, of course, is what the Mississippian, Frank Montgomery, had known before the charge was made, but he had been ignored when he tried to bring that information to the attention of his superiors. However, he is among the lucky survivors who make it back unscathed to the Rebel works. Afterwards, thinking back on their assault against the stalwart Yankee fortifications, he scornfully remarks that they were "literally filled with soldiers and it was impossible to hold what we had gained." As for ordering the charge in the first place, his feelings are clear, "I always thought and still think, somebody blundered."[7]

That somebody is none other than Old Grits himself, who now knows that Sherman's right is too strong to be attacked. Although it was Johnston's suspicion that the Yankees were not there in force, Bate was convicted of that same notion, and the blunder of the failed attack rests squarely on his shoulders. Realizing this,

John Logan (Prints and Photographs Division, Library of Congress, LC-DIG-cwpbh-03223)

he knows he can't repeat the mistake by sending his infantry on another foolhardy mission. He orders the battery not to signal the second charge, and written orders calling off the infantry advance are given to his couriers, who go running into the woods to find his three brigade commanders.[8] While word goes out canceling any further movement, some of the Confederate rank and file who are not on the front line, but are close enough to witness the countermand of the next attack, wonders why. They are low privates who have no idea of Johnston's battle plans to test the enemy's strength and little understanding of the menacing threat that Bate has just discovered in front of them. Sam Watkins, for instance, having watched the entire attack from his reserve position, believed the Rebel charge could have had a favorable outcome if properly supported. Thus, when he sees the survivors of Armstrong's brigade come streaming back, he questions the tactical wisdom of the commanders. "Why we were not ordered forward to follow up his success, I do not know," he dubiously remarks in his memoirs.[9]

But Bate knows. However, his orders to stop everything will soon be lost in a series of events that will amplify the mistake he's already made. The courier bearing Bate's message that the infantry should remain in their present position happens to find Thomas Smith commanding the brigade on Armstrong's immediate left. Yet the courier didn't find Smith where he was supposed to be. Eager to move out when he heard Armstrong's guns opening the attack, the impatient Smith had moved his troops from their original line forward "under the brow of the hill" immediately in their front, and then awaited the signal to advance. Unfortunately, Smith failed to inform the other two brigade commanders that he had moved into a new position.[10]

※※※※※※※※※※※※※※

Meanwhile, over on the right of Bate's line and farthest from the action, Joe Lewis and his Kentucky brigade are waiting for the signal to attack. Lewis is a tall, handsome man with blue eyes and a full moustache. Like Bate, he has earned the reputation of a strict disciplinarian, and at first blush, he strikes those around him as a rude and ornery character with a hair-triggered temper. But Lewis possesses another side, one that is compassionate and sensitive when it comes to the welfare of his troops. And unlike their feelings for the irascible Bate, they love the brigade commander. These Kentuckians are known throughout the army as the Orphan Brigade, and Lewis refers to them as "my Orphans." Most of them joined the Confederate army early in the war and have endured more than their fair share of hardships, fighting through numerous battles and gaining recognition as some of the best troops in the Army of Tennessee. Because Union forces have occupied their state from the time they left, most of them have never enjoyed the benefit of a furlough to go home. In effect, they've become exiles, separated from their homes and families, and hence deserving the bereaved yet suitably distinguished title of the Orphan Brigade.[11]

Near 4:00 P.M., while Armstrong is still pounding the Union right and Smith's brigade is easing up into a new position, Lewis and his Orphans are straining to hear the cannon shots that will signal them to advance. However the noise of Armstrong's guns is so loud that it's impossible to pick out the sound of the signal battery amidst the banging battle racket. Not only can't they hear, neither can the men see anything through the tangled undergrowth and trees. Lewis begins to worry that they have failed to hear the signal. The uncertainty causes him to send his adjutant, Capt. Fayette Hewitt, to learn whether or not they had indeed missed their cue to advance. Hewitt trots down the line, passing the Florida brigade and continues on until he arrives at the position where Thomas Smith's troops had been earlier. Finding only empty ditches, Hewitt assumes that Smith has already advanced, and the Kentuckians had just failed to hear the signal. His assumption, of course, is wrong, for Smith's brigade has moved just a short distance forward but is hidden in the dense forest. Unaware of their presence, he returns to Lewis informing him that Smith had already advanced and "that they were behind time."[12]

That said, Lewis orders his Orphan Brigade to climb out of their works and advance on the enemy. The Kentuckians are ready to go, having already removed their backpacks and any other baggage that might slow them down. They move forward through the woods and, after a short distance, emerge into an area of cleared underbrush where they find themselves alone, exposed on both flanks, and facing what appears to be the entire Federal XV Corps. "As soon as we came in sight of them," remembers Capt. John Weller, "we knew we had met them in vain." On they come, and although deadly fire pours into both their flanks, the Orphans manage to push through the first line of enemy ramparts, silence a battery, and plant their colors within fifty yards of the second and strongest Federal line.[13]

The Federals facing Lewis's brigade belong to the division of Peter Osterhaus. By this time, Osterhaus has returned from the Union far right, where he had led one of his brigades to assist Harrow in beating back Armstrong's attack. He arrives back just in time to see his battery of twelve-pound Napoleons "most excitedly engaged in repelling Rebel columns," and according to Osterhaus, those columns are being "mowed down by the hundred." His assessment of the Federal fire seems to agree with that of the charging Kentuckians, who later remarked that the Yankee line seemed like "a sheet of flame" pouring forth "a literal storm of shot and shell." This doesn't prevent the Orphan Brigade from working even closer. They nearly reach the second line of enemy works where they make a stubborn stand, taking cover behind anything that offers protection, including the bodies of their fellow Orphans, which are quickly piling up in heaps.[14]

While Lewis's troops struggle to hold their position, Finley's Florida brigade suddenly appears on their left, driving toward Morgan Smith's division of the XV Corps. Col. Robert Bullock is presently in command of the Floridians, replacing Finley, who is recovering from a wound received at Resaca. Like Lewis, Bullock has yet to receive word from Bate that the attack has been canceled. Misled by the uproar of the charges of both Armstrong and Lewis, Bullock has ordered still another attack, and from the Federals vantage point, it seems to be suicidal. "They came with heads bowed down and their hats pulled over their eyes as if to hide from view their inevitable death," is how Ohio private John Duke remembers the futile charge by Bullock. Withering fire from the entrenched Yankee line rips into the Florida brigade that is advancing in three lines. Watching their lines move forward, Duke believes the Rebels have stepped into a "death trap." Nevertheless, he's impressed with their tenacity. "It seemed as though nothing short of utter annihilation could stop them."[15]

Indeed, "utter annihilation" may have been their fate if Bate's courier had not found Bullock and delivered the message that the attack should not be made. Although their losses to this point are heavy, the Florida brigade is saved from a more serious disaster when Bullock orders them back to their works. The same cannot be said for the Orphan Brigade, which now stands alone and unsupported. By now, it's obvious the attack has failed, and Bate's order to retire finally arrives on the field. It's too late for many of the Orphans, but the regiments, one by one, begin to fall back through the smoke and murderous fire. All of them, that is, except the Fifth Kentucky. They are within twenty yards of the Federal breastworks and do not intend to give up the position they've labored so hard to gain. But realizing that to stay any longer would mean certain death, their commander, Col. Hiram Hawkins, grabs the regimental flag and leads his stubborn men from the field. Unfortunately, they are unable to recover their dead and wounded because of the severe shelling pouring into them from the Union works. The badly wounded Orphans, who can't drag themselves back through the underbrush, are left to linger among the corpses. There, some of them will remain for hours or even days before they can be moved.[16]

"The Brigade is terribly cut up," Johnny Jackman writes in his diary that night. Of the Kentucky regiments that Joe Lewis had led into the assault, their losses have been calculated to be as high as 51 percent. Added to those in Bullock's and Armstrong's brigades, Confederate casualties probably come close to 1,200 men, although an official and accurate account is never offered. Whatever the exact figure, it will certainly dwarf the Union losses, which General Logan reports as only 379. These lopsided numbers once again confirmed the absurdity of charging prepared breastworks, regardless of which side might be defending them. And this time, at the Battle of Dallas, fortified Union soldiers achieve the same bloody results that the Confederates had accomplished at Pickett's Mill.[17]

* * * * * * * * * * * * * *

This same night, around the campfires, Jackman listens to the railings of his fellow Kentuckians as they heap the blame for the disastrous attack on General Bate. Taking in their complaints about Old Grits, he records in his diary that "he catches it from all sides and quarters." Jackman finds it hard to disagree, saying, "The boys generally know what is in front of them, and could have told Gen. Bate better." Bate, after learning of the Kentuckians complaint against him, denies any such blunder and claims "the error was committed by another." This, of course, is in reference to the overzealous Capt. Fayette Hewitt, who had innocently volunteered bad information to Joe Lewis about not being "up to time" attacking the enemy. In his after-action report, Bate attempts to put a better face on the failed affair, boasting that "serious punishment" was inflicted on the enemy thus "weakening his resources." This assertion is, of course, nonsense, and no such opinion seems to support it within the ranks of his beaten and discouraged brigade.[18]

Over in the Union fortifications, however, there is a feeling of elation among the weary soldiers. They believe they've met and repulsed Hardee's entire corps in a series of fierce and sporadic attacks. Hardly had the last shots sputtered to a stop and silence fell on the field than a great cheer rang out from their lines. Later, in the darkness, Capt. Charles Wills makes his diary entry at 7:00 P.M.: "Talk about fighting, etc., we've seen it this P.M. sure, of all the interesting and exciting times on record this must take the palm."[19] It's true that the Battle of Dallas has been an exciting victory for the Union troops, especially those in John Logan's corps. However, from a tactical standpoint, nothing has changed. Logan's corps and the rest of McPherson's army wing on the Federal right are still pinned down, unable to make the shift eastward that Sherman has ordered.

Chapter Fourteen

What Is to Become of Us?

Throughout the night, Union soldiers remain vigilant, fearing another savage attack by the Confederates. This threat causes the worried McPherson to postpone the plan to shift his forces and link up with Thomas, and he sends word to Sherman; "I do not know how I can move tonight." The attack, however, never comes. The Confederates are still licking their wounds from the afternoon's fight and have no desire to add to their horrific losses. But the next morning, May 29, 1864, a Sunday, the skirmishing starts up again in earnest, causing the sleep-weary Union soldiers to believe that another attack is imminent.[1]

But there will be no more grand frontal attacks or massive charges against the flanks. Neither Sherman nor Johnston will again attempt another serious attack here, but neither one will retreat. Instead, the two armies will brace themselves for a standoff that will drag on for a week. They now find that they are facing a strange and static kind of warfare they've yet to experience. This new and terrifying style of fighting is the emergence of what becomes known as trench warfare, a consuming nightmare that will evolve from here on through the campaign and into the future, finally reaching its climax in the First World War. There will be no furious battles followed by huge body counts, but in many ways, it will be worse because a battle has an inevitable end. Here the killing and maiming, although less, will be constant and grinding, as each side will torment the other with artillery barrages, incessant sniping, and quick-striking night attacks by skirmishers. Making matters worse are the squalid conditions of the trenches, foul weather, junglelike terrain, and so on, causing the soldiers to doubt what possesses them to fight and die for such ground. Some of them will try to escape the misery by desertion, or by skulking to the rear where they pretend to be wounded or sick. Others cowardly maraud through the backwoods, pillaging the poor farms and hiding wherever they can. But most of them simply try to endure this purgatory they continue to describe as the Hell Hole.

※※※※※※※※※※※※※※

Since May 25, when the two armies had first come to grips in front of New Hope Church, their positions have not dramatically changed. From a point just south of the town of Dallas, their lines run in a northeastward direction, past the tiny church, and continue on slightly beyond the creek bordering the Pickett Settlement, a distance of some eight miles. All along this front, the forest has been torn to shreds by artillery and small arms fire, and the ground is covered in a labyrinth of holes and diggings of every description. Trenches, rifle pits, and complex breastworks protected by high mounds of dirt and stacked logs burrow and tunnel mile after mile across the wrecked landscape. Picks, spades, and shovels are in constant demand by the soldiers, and these tools are valued nearly as much as the weapons they carry. When circumstances require a regiment to change its position, men pack their entrenching tools atop mules and bring them along. After taking up a new position, "every man would dig in as though his life depended on his work," writes Sgt. Rice Bull, 123rd New York, adding for emphasis, "In many cases it did."[2]

Even after digging in, the soldiers are always in range of enemy snipers hiding in the treetops or thick underbrush, waiting for a head to bob above the breastworks. This alone is a terrible psychological burden. "I tell you it is a strain on a man's nerves," complains Captain Wills in his diary. And a Confederate private in Cheatham's division agrees and adds, "Really there is no safety within two miles of the battle field." Even those not in the proximity of the trenches and well behind the lines experience what an Alabama war correspondent describes as "the concert" of the sharpshooters. He writes his home paper: "For myself, when one of them whisks by my ear, I take it as very kind and complimentary that it came so far and no farther, and hail it evidence that my time has not yet arrived." For many, however, their time has arrived, with some units reporting losses of a dozen or more men a day to the deadly snipers.[3]

As the snipers continue their grim business of daily killings, the soldiers try to contend with the constant menace, but from privates to generals, all are mad about it. Georgia private William Norrell, for instance, shares his disgust in a diary entry dated May 30: "This picket firing is beneath the dignity of civilized warfare, as it accomplishes nothing but murder and has nothing to recommend it. No nation does it but ours and the Indian tribes we got it from that I know of. It is real *bushwhacking* and nothing else." And behind the Union lines General Sherman expresses the same concern, in somewhat the same way, in a letter to his brother. "It is a Big Indian War," he protests, relating in ire how the enemy sharpshooters "kill our wagoneers, messengers & couriers."[4]

Another favorite target of the snipers are the artillerymen whose batteries are sometimes exposed and vulnerable. Because the cannoneers are responsible for a good deal of the slaying and mutilations, sharpshooters are constantly called on to pick them off and silence their big guns. However, the batteries on either side are never quiet for long, lobbing their shells anytime and anywhere they think they can inflict some damage. "Three men had their heads carried away," laments one Alabama colonel after his regiment experiences a sudden cannonade from the Federal guns. During the times when the artillery barrages are especially heavy, it's a small wonder they don't claim more lives than they do. Indeed, they would, but the guns are often inaccurate—in the Confederate's motley arsenal, sometimes inferior—with ammunition malfunctions being the norm if not the rule. Thus, after Harrow's Federal division undergoes a severe bombardment, Captain Wills records, "The Rebels have just finished throwing 126 shells at us, only 19 of which bursted." Notwithstanding the times when the shells fail to explode and go ripping off through the woods or plow harmlessly into the mud, the cannon barrages are an effective tactic for both sides. It forces the soldiers to spend sleepless nights repairing and improving the fortifications against the penetrating solid shot. What's more, like the sniper fire, it grates on their nerves, causing the teeth-clenching troops to hunker down in the ditches and endure the screaming sounds of shells whining all around them.[5]

Nightfall brings on other problems for the soldiers, not the least of which are confusion and fear. Under the cover of darkness, each side will typically send out skirmishers to drive back the enemy pickets, and then attempt to surprise and overrun some section of their breastworks. This rarely succeeds, however, and usually only results in flashes of frightening rifle and cannon fire, momentary chaos, and men becoming turned around and lost in the dense woods where prisoners are taken by both sides.

Such an episode occurs on the night of May 29 at 10:00 P.M., about the time that McPherson is once again attempting to move his troops to the left. Just minutes before the infantry movement is to get underway, wild-eyed Union pickets come plunging back through the dark woods, screaming that a Rebel attack is on the way. Gunfire subsequently erupts all along the Yankee lines in front of John Logan and Grenville Dodge's troops. There is, of course, no real attack being made, but this sudden outburst along the Federal front ignites a similar reaction from the Confederate lines held by Bate's division and Cleburne's troops, who have now been returned to Hardee's corps after their victory at Pickett's Mill. Both sides now believe they are under attack, and the firing continues throughout the night in a series of imagined assaults. Why the Union pickets had ever believed an attack was in progress is unclear. They may have been aroused by small bands of Rebels sallying out in the night to recover their dead and wounded from the previous afternoon's fight. Or too much whiskey may have produced their fantasy. "Some say," according to Johnny Jackman, "the Federal skirmishers got drunk and turned around so completely that they commenced firing on their own works." In addition, Capt. Sam Foster agrees with that explanation, writing in his diary, "The heavy fireing [sic] on our left was the Yanks firing on their own pickets. Their pickets came over to our line for protection from their own men—They reported that they were all drunk over there."[6]

No doubt John Barleycorn did play a part in stirring the imaginations and overreactions of the Yankee soldiers, but it's doubtful that drunkenness was the sole cause of so many wild outbursts. Repeatedly throughout the night, edgy Union soldiers open up with devastating fire for no apparent reason. Pvt. J. P. Cannon and thirty of his comrades from the Twenty-seventh Alabama may have been suspects in causing at least one of the uproars from the skittish Yankee guns. "Last night our turn came for picket duty," he logs in his journal on May 30, 1864. His company has moved through the woods to a position near the Federal breastworks, taking care not to make a sound along the way. Everything is quiet, going as planned until "some of the boys got tangled up in a brush pile, making considerable racket." That clumsy mishap opens up the gates of hell. "Without warning, boom! boom! boom!, a battery of six guns not more than 200 yards distant opened on us and fairly shook the earth." After the initial shock, while the woods are still boiling in smoke and everyone is hugging the ground, "the infantry rose from their trenches and a sheet of flame burst from their ranks. It reminded us of one of the roaring winds, the flashes of lightning and heavy peals of thunder in a terrible storm. The night was dark but the woods above and around us were ablaze with burning fuses and bursting shells." For Cannon, such a violent display of Yankee firepower strikes him as a bit superfluous: "Five thousand guns and 20 cannons shooting right into our little squad of 30 men! Would they ever cease?"[7]

Whatever actually triggered the events of this long night's hullabaloo only amounts, in the words of Thomas Mackall, a lieutenant on Johnston's staff, to a "great waste of ammunition . . . both sides aroused by false alarm." Everyone, however, is exhausted, as the firing does not cease until just before daylight without either side gaining any advantage. "I don't know when I have been so used up as this morning, and the whole command is not far from the same condition," writes a weary Captain Wills. And while he admits, "these night fights are very grand," he points out "there was a good deal more shooting than hitting on both sides."[8]

When daylight finally breaks, the skirmishers return to the safety of their trenches, and everyone does their best to stay concealed. Because of the trenches' proximity, in some cases less than one hundred yards apart, the armies can hear the cursing conversations of their enemy across the way. At times, one side or the other will attempt to coax the enemy soldiers out in the open, usually by some means of chicanery. One such ruse is pulled off by the Forty-sixth Ohio from the ditches near Dallas.

Here, according to Cpl. John Clemson, the Ohioans decide to stage a fake charge. On a given signal, bugles blow and the soldiers begin yelling at the top of their lungs as if an attack is beginning. As expected, heads from the Confederate works begin to rise up to meet the charge, only to discover a galling fire from well-aimed Spencer rifles, killing and wounding many of them. The Southerners find small humor in such a dastardly trick and dive back in their holes. When the firing dies away, a Yankee rifleman hollers, "Say Johnny, how many of you are over there?" After a long pause, some scarecrow Confederate yells back, "Well I guess there's enough for another killin."[9]

****

As the days and nights drag by, the soldiers of both armies face a variety of tribulations. The weather, for instance, turns almost tropical with sporadic downpours of rain falling in torrents. Always wet, their heavy wool uniforms never completely dry out. Either they're soaked by the pelting thunderstorms or they're damp from sweating in the steamy ditches. "It did not rain continuously," recalls Union sergeant Rice Bull, "but during some part of every day it hit us, usually thunderstorms of the most violent sort." As a result, the trenches are flooded, leaving thousands of men standing knee deep in the slimy, red mud.[10]

Adding to the misery, sanitary conditions become unbearable. The air is heavy with a mixture of sickening odors. The stench of human and animal excrement surrounds the men and mingles with the clouds of sulfurous gun smoke that hang dirty and yellow over the ditches and in the treetops. But for the soldiers, the smell of death is far worse. William Nugent, a Mississippi soldier, describes the revolting odor in a home letter: "The great number of dead horses, mules and human beings, makes the air extremely offensive in the vicinity of the trenches." Due to the constant firing, the men can't risk moving from the trenches to dispose of the swollen, fly-covered carcasses, and Nugent goes on to say how anxious he is to "get away from this big army and breathe a little fresh air."[11]

Somehow, because there's really no choice, the men get used

to the weather and suffocating stench. More troubling and harder to handle, however, are the insects, which include swarms of mosquitoes and flies, joined by the crawling variety, all of which drive the men wild. Lice, especially, are an ever-present plague, and the soldiers spend fitful hours slapping and snatching them off their bodies. "Ursula, there is no chance to keep clean," writes Sgt. Joel Murphree, Fifty-seventh Alabama, to his wife, "I am as dirty as a hog and nearly as lousy." Across the way in the Federal works, Lt. Col. Sam Merrill, in a letter to his wife, echoes the same complaint for the same reasons. "One of the horrors of this kind of war is that the men's bodies and clothes are alive and nothing can be done to relieve them as they have no change of clothing and seldom any opportunity to bathe. Everyone from colonel to private is broken out horribly, and cannot enjoy a moment's rest for the intolerable itching."[12]

Taken all together, the incessant fighting, bad weather, filth, stench, vermin, and other by-products of the harsh trench life create a breed of soldiers who are broken down and horribly disgusting. When prisoners are taken, both sides are revolted by the appearance of their enemy. After some Rebel soldiers of the Twentieth Georgia are captured, Charles Wills remarks in his diary, "I never saw such a dirty, greasy, set of mortals," all of whom, incidentally, "had whiskey in his canteen." By the same token, William Nugent sees the Union prisoners in much the same way, nothing more than "miserable specimens of humanity," adding in disgust, "their clothes are filthy, torn & greasy and their persons are very offensive."[13]

Ordinarily, Confederates who are taken prisoner could at least look forward to the prospect of a decent meal from their captors. Here in the Hell Hole, however, the Yankees are no better off than the hungry Southerners, and probably worse. They've been on half-rations since leaving the railroad at Kingston, and their animals are existing on leaves and plants as their only fodder. "My horses are absolutely dying from starvation. Five from one company dropped on picket this morning, totally exhausted for want of something to eat," complains E. M. McCook, a Union cavalry colonel, to his commanding officer. Since their mounts are starving, some of the Union cavalry units around Dallas, according to Rebel scouts and local farmers, begin to abandon their positions and move to the rear in search of forage for their horses. Expecting them to remain in place as a viable fighting force under such conditions would be useless. Consequently, Colonel McCook warns his commander, "I tell you their condition now so that you may not rely on the division as serviceable, for it certainly is not."[14]

* * * * * * * * * * * * * * *

By now Sherman sees his army as being stretched to the limits of its endurance and knows they must break out of the deadlock and return to the rail line. But McPherson, in spite of several attempts, has not been able to leave his fortifications and link up with Thomas, thereby enabling the rest of the army to move. On May 30, Sherman decides to take a personal hand in the matter. "I will go down myself to-day," he writes John Schofield, "and see if that force cannot come up to us to enable us to work around to the east and north." Although Sherman claims he dutifully visits "all parts of our lines nearly every day," he also admits that he rarely sees many of the enemy soldiers, except for "skirmishers dodging from tree to tree." Today, however, after riding to McPherson's lines, he experiences a close call with his hidden enemy. While Sherman is standing with McPherson, Logan, and some of his own staff, a Rebel sharpshooter's bullet grazes Logan's arm then hits one of his staff officers "square in the breast." That disturbing moment serves as another reminder for Sherman that he is fighting an Indian war in the middle of "as difficult country as was ever fought over by civilized armies."[15]

To remove his army from this country is becoming Sherman's most pressing concern and his sole purpose in spending the day examining McPherson's position. After the inspection, he returns to his headquarters and writes McPherson the next morning; "You will observe that after full reflection and due observation I have concluded to make the movement by the left." So that's that; Sherman has made up his mind that McPherson will begin moving out on the night of May 31.What's more, he tells him exactly how it will be done. His instructions are implicit, extracting "division by division" with one screening the movement of the next until the entire XV and XVI Corps are linked to Thomas and the army is reunited. In case McPherson has any apprehension, Sherman assures him that the Confederates will be "easily repulsed" should they follow and try to stop him. Then taking one last precaution, he sends McPherson a map this same afternoon, drawing out the breakaway as he has designed it to happen.[16]

Meantime, Sherman gives instructions to his other army commanders, George Thomas and John Schofield, as to their roles in the movement. Finally, he directs the worn-out cavalry divisions of George Stoneman and Kenner Garrard to secure the rail line from Allatoona Pass southward to the town of Acworth where he intends the army to ultimately emerge from the Hell Hole and reconnect with the railroad. Although these cavalrymen have been in the saddle for days and their horses are dropping from starvation, the fiery redhead is adamant in his orders, telling Garrard, "Force your way into and through the pass along the railroad . . . the success of our movement depends on our having Allatoona Pass."[17]

And so in the dark of night, on May 31, McPherson begins moving his army wing, slowly disengaging them from the grip they've been held in for so many days. The silent march continues through the morning of June 1, when the leading elements finally make contact with Thomas and the Army of the Cumberland. "It was ticklish business moving out from under at least 30 of the enemy's guns," confesses Captain Wills in his diary, "and we did it very quietly." Marching northeast through the dense woods, McPherson's troops pass the scene of the first day's battle at New Hope Church, where Wills sees for the first time the awful results of that brawl. "The woods are all torn up with canister, shell and shot, and bloody shoes, clothing and accouterments are thick," he enters in his diary. Surprisingly, the little Methodist church is still standing but is badly scarred from the cannon shot and musketry. Next to the church, in the small cemetery where Stovall's Georgians had made their stand, the ground is torn up, headstones overturned, and the picket fences separating the graves ripped up by the soldiers. The most disturbing reminder of the ordeal, however, are the unburied corpses that still remain here, rotting on the ground between the lines.[18]

Abandoned Confederate breastworks, from The Photographic History of the Civil War, *1911, 3:113*

****

McPherson's withdrawal is successful. From the ditches on the Confederate front, the Yankee movement goes undetected. But on the morning of June 1, Rebel cavalrymen atop Elsberry Mountain begin sending word to Johnston of a mass exodus of "heavy columns of infantry" and "wagons three miles off passing continually." Alarmed by these reports, Old Joe rides to the mountain around noon, only to see a trail of dust marking the enemy's escape. Perhaps because he believes it's too late, or perhaps because he has been anticipating this inevitable shift in the Federal lines, Johnston orders no attack or pursuit. And by now, he's heard the distressing news that Union cavalry have managed to drive away the paltry Rebel resistance at the railroad, opening the way for Sherman to reach that vital point.[19]

The next morning, June 2, the rain is pouring and the

skirmishing and sniping once again resumes all along the front. At the same time, Sherman continues sidling his army to the left toward the railroad while Johnston, it seems, is either unwilling or unable to stop him. Whatever the case, it appears no further attempt will be made. On the other hand, Johnston is apparently not entirely displeased. He already considers the events of the past week to be an amalgamated victory of sorts and has inferred this in a telegram sent to Bragg yesterday, the same day McPherson had escaped from his grip. In that wire, he tells Bragg that in the army's "partial engagements it has had great advantage, and the sum of all the combats amounts to a battle." After all, he has reports from one of his sources that Sherman has suffered between 8,000 and 10,000 casualties on their present line, a figure that's surely too high, but one he chooses to believe. The ever-sinister Bragg is unimpressed with the army's "partial engagements," telling him so in a return wire that drips with the intimation that when compared to Robert E. Lee, who "has greatly damaged the enemy" in Virginia, Johnston is not getting the job done. Johnston, as usual, seems unmoved by the criticism coming out of Richmond, which is evident when he ignores Bragg's cheap innuendo. Instead, he will continue to embrace his customary defensive strategy, and he calls a council of war with his three corps commanders, John Bell Hood, Leonidas Polk, and William Hardee, to discuss the army's next move.[20]

The meeting takes place at the small deserted cabin of the Widow Wigley near New Hope Church. The dwelling, such as it is, has been Johnston's headquarters for the last few days. Here Johnston concedes to his lieutenants that the New Hope-Dallas line will have to be abandoned. In other words, Johnston is ordering another retreat in a continuing series of retreats, and he's only about twenty-five miles from the gates of Atlanta. Hood, who offers the only account of this gathering and citing it as "historical fact," says the four generals were "assembled alone at night." According to the big Kentuckian, "General Johnston suggested Macon as being the place to fall back upon," and then notes that the proposal "was received in silence." After the meeting ends, and Hood, Polk, and Hardee are riding back to their respective headquarters, the three generals are overcome with depression at the thought of retreating all the way to Macon, which is about one hundred miles beyond Atlanta. Before separating, Hood remembers their mutual sentiment when one of them asks, "In the name of Heaven, what is to become of us?"[21]

The Army of Tennessee retreats on the night of June 4, 1864, to Lost Mountain, which is roughly six miles southeast of their present line, a far cry from the place Hood had claimed to be his commander's destination. Sloshing through the rain and red Georgia mud on what Sam Foster describes as "the darkest night of all the dark nights," they leave the Hell Hole behind. As they go, that same haunting question pondered by their generals must surely be echoing through the minds of the mud-streaked soldiers: "In the name of Heaven, what is to become of us?"[22]

Notes

Chapter One

1. U.S. War Department, *The War of the Rebellion: A Compilation of the Official Records of the Union and Confederate Armies* (Washington, D.C.: Government Printing Office, 1880-1901), ser. 1, vol. 32, pt. 3: 550-72. Hereafter, this source will be cited as OR, and all references being to series 1 unless otherwise indicated. Whenever a volume consists of two or more parts, the volume number will precede the OR followed by the part number.

2. David Evans, *Sherman's Horsemen: Union Cavalry Operations in the Atlanta Campaign* (Bloomington: Indiana University Press, 1996), xxii-xxiii; Albert Castel, *Decision in the West: The Atlanta Campaign of 1864* (Lawrence, KS: University Press of Kansas, 1992), 39.

3. Joseph T. Glatthaar, *Partners in Command: The Relationships Between Leaders in the Civil War* (New York: The Free Press, 1994), 137.

4. Castel, *Decision in the West*, 68.

5. 38 OR 4:299.

6. William T. Sherman, *Memoirs of General W. T. Sherman* (New York: Literary Classics of the United States, Inc., 1990), 511.

7. *Mobile Daily Advertiser and Register*, 7 June 1864.

8. Sherman, *Memoirs*, 511.

9. W. T. Sherman to Ellen, May 20, 1864, Sherman Family Papers, University of Notre Dame, Notre Dame, Indiana.

10. Sherman, *Memoirs*, 374.

11. W. T. Sherman to John, May 26, 1864, Sherman Papers, Library of Congress, Washington, D.C.

12. Richard M. McMurry, *Atlanta, 1864* (Lincoln: University of Nebraska Press, 2000), 85-86; Castel, *Decision in the West*, 218.

13. 38 OR 4:299.

14. 52 OR 1:622.

15. 38 OR 4:299.

16. Ibid.; Sherman, *Memoirs*, 512.

17. Oliver O. Howard, "The Struggle for Atlanta," in *Battles and Leaders of the Civil War*, ed. Robert U. Johnson and Clarence C. Buel, vol.4 (1887; reprint, Edison, NJ: Castle, n.d.), 306; Charles W. Wills, *Army Life of an Illinois Soldier* (Washington, D.C.: Globe Printing Co., 1906), 246.

18. W. T. Sherman to Ellen, May 22, 1864, Sherman Family Papers, University of Notre Dame, Notre Dame, Indiana.

19. Castel, *Decision in the West*, 131-32, 220.

20. Ibid., 220.

Chapter Two

1. Sam Watkins, *Company Aytch: Or, a Sideshow of the Big Show* (1882; reprint, New York: Collier Books, 1962), 101.

2. Craig L. Symonds, *Joseph E. Johnston: A Civil War Biography* (New York: W. W. Norton & Company, 1992), 10, 49-52.

3. Thomas L. Connelly, *Autumn of Glory: The Army of Tennessee 1862-1865* (Baton Rouge: Louisiana State University Press, 1971), 281-83; Castel, *Decision in the West*, 28-30.

4. Mary Chesnut, *Mary Chesnut's Civil War*, ed. C. Vann Woodward (New Haven: Yale University Press, 1981), 482-83.

5. Castel, *Decision in the West*, 29; Symonds, *Joseph E. Johnston*, 89-90, 125-39 passim; Glatthaar, *Partners in Command*, 95-133 passim.

6. Connelly, *Autumn of Glory*, 281-86.

7. Judith Lee Hallock, *Braxton Bragg and Confederate Defeat*, vol. 2 (Tuscaloosa: University of Alabama Press, 1991), 1-6, (Bragg quoted, 25-26).

8. St. John Richardson Liddell, *Liddell's Record*, ed. Nathaniel Cheairs Hughes, Jr. (Baton Rouge: Louisiana State University Press, 1985), 106.

9. Grady McWhiney, *Braxton Bragg and Confederate Defeat*, vol. 1 (Tuscaloosa: University of Alabama Press, 1969), 379-88; Symonds, *Joseph E. Johnston*, 196-99.

10. Joseph E. Johnston, "Opposing Sherman's Advance to Atlanta," in *Battles and Leaders of the Civil War*, ed. Robert U. Johnson and Clarence C. Buel, vol. 4 (1887; reprint, Edison, NJ: Castle, n.d.), 260; Castel, *Decision in the West*, 31.

11. Castel, *Decision in the West*, 33-34; Watkins, *Company Aytch*, 102; Noel Crowson and John V. Brogden, comps., *Bloody Banners and Barefoot Boys: A History of the 27th Regiment Alabama Infantry, CSA: The Civil War Memoirs and Diary Entries of J. P. Cannon M.D.* (Shippensburg, PA: Burd Street Press, 1997; White Mane Publishing Company, Inc.), 66.

12. Quoted in Christopher Losson, *Tennessee's Forgotten Warriors: Frank Cheatham and His Confederate Division* (Knoxville: University of Tennessee Press, 1989), 135.

13. Ibid.; Symonds, *Joseph E. Johnston*, 386.

14. 32 OR 3:801, 865-66. Official Returns are somewhat confusing since they are presented in several categories. For example, "Effectives total present" does not include officers, only enlisted men who are combat-ready, while "Aggregate present" includes officers as well as supporting personnel such as cooks, clerks, engineers, musicians, teamsters, hospital orderlies, and a host of other supernumeraries.

15. Stanley F. Horn, *The Army of Tennessee* (Norman, OK: University of Oklahoma Press, 1953), 324-25; Larry J. Daniel, *Cannoneers in Gray: The Field Artillery of the Army of Tennessee, 1861-1865* (Tuscaloosa: University of Alabama Press, 1984), 148.

16. Watkins, *Company Aytch*, 143.

17. F. Jay Taylor, ed., *Reluctant Rebel: The Secret Diary of Robert Patrick 1861-1865* (Baton Rouge: Louisiana State University Press, 1959), 166-67.

18. 38 OR 4:735.

19. 38 OR 4:725, 736.

20. Johnston's letters to Lydia, May 21 and 23, 1864, quoted in Symonds, *Joseph E. Johnston*, 295-96.

21. Johnston's baptism and Lydia Johnston's quote in letter to Polk dated May 16, 1864, in Symonds, *Joseph E. Johnston*, 290.

22. 38 OR 4:742.

Chapter Three

1. Rice C. Bull, *Soldiering: The Civil War Diary of Rice C. Bull,* ed. K. Jack Bauer (San Rafael, CA: Presido Press, 1978), 112-19.

2. Alexis Cope, *The Fifteenth Ohio Volunteers and Its Campaigns, War of 1861-65* (Columbus, OH: Press of the Edward T. Miller Co., 1916), 446-76.

3. 38 OR 2:122-23.

4. W. T. Sherman to Ellen, July 29, 1864, Sherman Family Papers, University of Notre Dame, Notre Dame, Indiana.

5. Castel, *Decision in the West,* 94-97; Hooker's letter to a friend quoted in Castel, 97.

6. 38 OR 2:122-23; Castel, *Decision in the West,* 221. The uncharted road that Hooker mistakenly takes is known today as the Old Cartersville Road.

7. 38 OR 2:123; 38 OR 3:843.

8. 38 OR 2:123.

9. Sherman, *Memoirs,* 794; 38 OR 4:507.

10. 38 OR 1:862; Sherman quoted in Castel, *Decision in the West,* 223.

11. Chesnut, *Mary Chesnut's Civil War,* 565.

12. Ibid., 559. For sources drawn from detailing Hood's character, appearance, and relationships with Jefferson Davis and Sally Buchanan Preston, see Richard M. McMurry, *John Bell Hood and the War for Southern Independence* (Lexington: University Press of Kentucky, 1982); Connelly, *Autumn of Glory,* 321-22; Wiley Sword, *The Confederacy's Last Hurrah: Spring Hill, Franklin, and Nashville* (Lawrence, KS: University Press of Kansas, 1992), 6-13, 23-29; James Lee McDonough and Thomas L Connelly, *Five Tragic Hours: The Battle Of Franklin* (Knoxville: University of Tennessee Press, 1983), 3-18 passim.

13. 38 OR 4:741

14. 38 OR 3:761, 833, 843-44.

15. 38 OR 3:843-44.

16. Ibid.

17. Sam Davis Elliott, *Soldier of Tennessee: General Alexander P. Stewart and the Civil War in the West* (Baton Rouge: Louisiana State University Press, 1999), 7-10, 18-19, 27, 70-71, 80, 304-5.

18. Ibid., 184; 38 OR 3:813, 818, 833, 848.

19. Bromfield L. Ridley, *Battles and Sketches of the Army of Tennessee* (1906; reprint, Dayton, OH: Morningside Bookshop, 1995), 303.

Chapter Four

1. 38 OR 1:66; 38 OR 2:30, 123; Castel, *Decision in the West,* 223-26.

2. Alpheus S. Williams, *From the Cannon's Mouth: The Civil War Letters of General Alpheus S. Williams,* ed. Milo M. Quaife (Lincoln: University of Nebraska Press, 1995), 312; 38 OR 2:30.

3. Bull, *Soldiering,* 112-19.

4. 38 OR 2:75; Williams, *From the Cannon's Mouth,* 313.

5. Williams, *From the Cannon's Mouth,* 313; 38 OR 2:31, 75.

6. 38 OR 2:382.

7. Castel, *Decision in the West,* 225; Samuel Merrill, *The Seventieth Indiana Volunteer Infantry in the War of the Rebellion* (Indianapolis: The Bowen-Merrill Co., 1900), 117-19.

8. 38 OR 3:833, 846.

9. Caruthers Stewart quoted in Elliott, *Soldier of Tennessee*, 188-89; Ridley, *Battles and Sketches*, 304.

10. Crowson and Brogden, *Bloody Banners,* 68.

11. Cope, *The Fifteenth Ohio Volunteers*, 446-76; Daniel, *Cannoneers in Gray*, 148.

12. *Memphis (Atlanta) Daily Appeal*, 27 May 1864; Patrick, *Reluctant Rebel*, 169.

13. 38 OR 3:761; 38 OR 2:123; Daniel, *Cannoneers in Gray*, 148; Ridley, *Battles and Sketches*, 304.

14. Daniel, *Cannoneers in Gray*, 148.

15. Ridley, *Battles and Sketches*, 304; Robert Howe, "Dead at New Hope Church," *Confederate Veteran* 5, no. 10 (October 1897). Included in this article is a wartime poem, from a collection by John Altgustin called "War Flowers," in which the ordeal of the Brigdens family is described in some detail by the poet.

16. Bull, *Soldiering*, 112-19.

17. Hiram Smith Williams, *This War So Horrible: The Civil War Diary of Hiram Smith Williams*, ed. Lewis N. Wynne and Robert A. Taylor (Tuscaloosa: University of Alabama Press, 1993), 81-82.

Chapter Five

1. John W. Tuttle, *The Union, the Civil War and John W. Tuttle: A Kentucky Captain's Account*, ed. Hambleton Tapp and James C. Klotter (Frankfort, KY: Kentucky Historical Society, 1980), 186-87; Cope, *The Fifteenth Ohio*, 446-76.

2. Tuttle, *The Union*, 186-87; Howard, "The Struggle for Atlanta," 306-7.

3. 38 OR 1:193; Howard, "The Struggle for Atlanta," 306.

4. W. T. Sherman to Ellen, July 29, 1864, Sherman Family Papers, University of Notre Dame, Notre Dame, Indiana; Ezra J. Warner, *Generals In Blue: Lives of the Union Commanders* (Baton Rouge: Louisiana State University Press, 1964 and 1992), 237-39.

5. Castel, *Decision in the West*, 98; Williams, *From the Cannon's Mouth*, 313. As promised, the sketch of Williams's advance appears in *Harper's Weekly* on July 2, 1864, see Williams, *From the Cannon's Mouth,* 357 n. 5.

6. McMurry, *Atlanta 1864*, 89; Hooker to Williams, October 31, 1864, in Williams, *From the Cannon's Mouth*, 349-50; 38 OR 2:14.

7. 38 OR 4:312; Sherman, *Memoirs,* 513.

8. Bull, *Soldiering*, 112-19.

9. Crowson and Brogden, *Bloody Banners,* 69; Williams, *This War So Horrible,* 81-82; 38 OR 3:818.

10. Douglas Hale, *The Third Texas Cavalry in the Civil War* (Norman, OK: University of Oklahoma Press, 1993), 122, 222. For an interesting study of the medical corps of the Army of Tennessee and the care provided in treating sickness, disease, and wounds, see Larry J. Daniel, *Soldiering in the Army of Tennessee: A Portrait of Life in a Confederate Army* (Chapel Hill: University of North Carolina Press, 1991), 64-82.

11. Watkins, *Company Aytch*, 137-38.

12. Quoted in Hale, *The Third Texas Cavalry*, 222.

13. Williams, *This War So Horrible*, 82-83.

14. Daniel, *Soldiering in the Army of Tennessee*, 152-53; Williams, *This War So Horrible*, 151 n. 38.

15. Warner, *Generals in Blue*, 62-63. There are no official lyrics to *Taps*. This verse is but one of the anonymous but popular ones passed down over the years.

Chapter Six

1. Symonds, *Joseph Johnston*, 298; 38 OR 4:742; 38 OR 3:761.
2. Elliot, *Soldier of Tennessee*, 189, 194.
3. Sherman, *Memoirs*, 513.
4. Castel, *Decision in the West*, 228-29; McMurry, *Atlanta 1864*, 89-90.
5. 38 OR 4:331.
6. 38 OR 4:317; Sherman, *Memoirs*, 513.
7. Horn, *The Army of Tennessee*, 331; Castel, *Decision in the West*, 228.
8. Spillard F. Horral, *History of the Forty-Second Indiana Volunteer Infantry* (Chicago: Donohue and Henneberry, 1892), 283.
9. Ibid.
10. John W. Clemson, "Surprised the Johnnies," *The National Tribune*, 30 September 1897.
11. Mamie Yeary, comp., *Reminiscences of the Boys in Gray, 1861-1865* (Dayton, OH: Morningside House, 1986), 414.
12. William Norrell, Norrell Diary, May 26, 1864, Kennesaw Mountain National Battlefield Park Library, Kennesaw, Georgia.
13. Crowson and Brogden, *Bloody Banners*, 70.
14. Mark H. Dunkleman and Michael J. Winey, eds. *An Illustrated History of the 154th Regiment, New York State Infantry Volunteers* (Rutherford, NJ: Fairleigh Dickinson University Press, 1981), 117.
15. Yeary, *Reminiscences of the Boys in Gray*, 355-58.
16. Henry Fales Perry, *History of the Thirty-Eighth Regiment Indiana Volunteer Infantry* (Palo Alto: F.A. Stuart, 1906), 135-38; Watkins, *Company Aytch*, 139.
17. William L. Nugent, *My Dear Nellie: The Civil War Letters of William L. Nugent to Eleanor Smith Nugent,* ed. William M. Cash and Lucy Somerville Howorth (Jackson: University Press of Mississippi, 1977), 182.
18. 38 OR 4:323.

Chapter Seven

1. 38 OR 3:706.
2. 38 OR 3:95, 278, 380; 38 OR 4:326-27; Losson, *Tennessee's Forgotten Warriors*, 149; Castel, *Decision in the West*, 231.
3. 38 OR 1:377.
4. Castel, *Decision in the West*, 229.
5. 38 OR 1:864.
6. Gregory C. McDermott, "A Fierce Hour at New Hope Church," *National Tribune*, 28 October 1897; Cope, *The Fifteenth Ohio Volunteers*, 446-76.
7. 38 OR 1:194, 377, 865.
8. 38 OR 4:324.
9. 38 OR 1:865; 38 OR 4:326.
10. "Family History of the Pickett Ancestors," Pickett's Mill Battlefield State Park Library, Dallas, Georgia.
11. 38 OR 1:194,195, 377.
12. 38 OR 3:705, 724; 38 OR 4:324, 742.
13. Daniel, *Soldiering in the Army of Tennessee*, 3-4; Horn, *The Army of Tennessee*, 314, 468 n.
14. Samuel T. Foster, *One of Cleburne's Command: The Civil War Reminiscences and Diary of Capt. Samuel T. Foster, Granbury's Texas Brigade,*

CSA, ed. Norman D. Brown (Austin: University of Texas Press, 1980), 81-82. During the Atlanta Campaign, a number of the Georgia troops present are either new conscripts or state militia who were reluctant to volunteer for wartime service and lack the experience and grit necessary to stand the pressure of hostile fire. The same cannot be said for the veteran Georgia soldiers such as those from Stovall's brigade who had fought so valiantly in the cemetery at New Hope Church.

Chapter Eight

1. Mauriel Phillips Joslyn, "A Moral and Upright Man," in *A Meteor Shining Brightly: Essays on Maj. Gen. Patrick Cleburne*, ed. Mauriel Phillips Joslyn (Milledgeville, GA: Terrell House Publishing, 1998), 186-88, (Conyngham and Arkansas private quoted, 187 and 188, respectively).

2. Sword, *The Confederacy's Last Hurrah*, 14-22 passim; Craig L. Symonds, *Stonewall of the West: Patrick Cleburne and the Civil War* (Lawrence, KS: University Press of Kansas, 1997), 32-33, 182-83, (Cleburne to brother Robert quoted, 187).

3. Symonds, *Stonewall of the West*, 32-33, 182-91, 194-95 (Cleburne quoted on 187); Sword, *The Confederacy's Last Hurrah*, 40.

4. Nash quoted in Joslyn, "A Moral and Upright Man," 190.

5. Symonds, *Stonewall of the West*, 192; Nathaniel Cheairs Hughes, Jr., *General William J. Hardee: Old Reliable* (Baton Rouge: Louisiana State University Press, 1965), 186-89.

6. Symonds, *Stonewall of the West*, 192-93, 197-98, (Cleburne quoted, 198); *Mobile Daily Advertiser and Register*, 15, 22, and 24 January 1864.

7. 38 OR 3:724; 38 OR 4:744.

8. Philip L. Secrist, *Sherman's 1864 Trail of Battle to Atlanta* (Macon, GA: Mercer University Press, 2006), 80; Foster, *One of Cleburne's Command*, 82.

9. 38 OR 3:724-25; 38 OR 3:948.

10. Frederick H. Bohmfalk, "Cleburne's Victory at the Pickett Settlement," in *A Meteor Shining Brightly*, ed. Mauriel Phillips Joslyn (Milledgeville, GA: Terrell House Publishing, 1998), 217-18; Symonds, *Stonewall of the West*, 127.

11. Foster, *One of Cleburne's Command*, 82-83; 38 OR 3:724.

Chapter Nine

1. Richard O'Connor, *Ambrose Bierce: A Biography* (Boston: Little, Brown & Company, 1967), 10-16, 39.

2. Ambrose Bierce, "The Crime at Pickett's Mill," in *The Collected Works of Ambrose Bierce* (New York: Gordian Press, 1966), 279-96.

3. Ibid.

4. Peter Cozzens, *This Terrible Sound: The Battle of Chickamauga* (Chicago: University of Illinois Press, 1994), 357-67.

5. Bierce, "The Crime at Pickett's Mill."

6. Ibid.

7. Ibid.

8. Daniel, *Soldiering in the Army of Tennessee*, 20. Daniel's chapter "Certainly a Rough Looking Set" (11-22) provides an interesting contrast between the armies of the Confederacy. Just as cultural differences existed between the western soldiers in the Army of Tennessee and their eastern counterparts in the Army of Northern Virginia, so too were there geographical distinctions evident in the troops of the Northern armies. Midwesterners, for example, coming from agrarian backgrounds tended to have more in common with the Southerners in

the Army of Tennessee than with their fellow soldiers hailing from the industrial east. Whether they were tougher soldiers, as the western Rebels claimed, is only a point of debate. John Bowers, *Chickamauga and Chattanooga: The Battles That Doomed the Confederacy* (New York: Avon Books, Inc., 1994), 8-10.

9. Bierce, "The Crime at Pickett's Mill."

10. Ibid.

11. Ibid.

12. Castel, *Decision in the West*, 233.

13. 38 OR 1:423; 38 OR 3:725; Mary A. H. Gay, *Life in Dixie During the Civil War,* ed. J. H. Segars (1892; reprint, Macon, GA: Mercer University Press, 2001), 89.

14. 38 OR 3:725; Bierce, "The Crime at Pickett's Mill."

15. Yeary, *Reminiscences of the Boys in Gray*, 17-19.

16. William J. Oliphant, *Only A Private: A Texan Remembers the Civil War: The Memoirs of William J. Oliphant*, ed. James M. McCaffrey (Houston: Halcyon Press, 2004), 64-65.

17. 38 OR 3:725.

18. Mark P. Lowery, "General Mark P. Lowery, an Autobiography," *Kennesaw Gazette*, 15 November 1888.

19. McDermott, "A Fierce Hour at New Hope Church."

20. 38 OR 1:195.

21. Phillip L. Secrist, "Scenes of Awful Carnage," *Civil War Times Illustrated* (June 1971).

Chapter Ten

1. 38 OR 1:378.

2. Cope, *The Fifteenth Ohio Volunteers and Its Campaigns*, 450-73.

3. Ibid.

4. 38 OR 1:865-66; 38 OR 4:327, 333-34. *Official Records* show Thomas's note to Howard (38 OR 4:333-34) as dated May 28 rather than May 27, an obvious mistake.

5. Cope, *The Fifteenth Ohio Volunteers and Its Campaigns,* 450-73.

6. Ibid.; Castel, *Decision in the West*, 238-39.

7. 38 OR 1:594-95; Perry, *History of the Thirty Eighth Regiment Indiana Volunteer Infantry*, 135-38. Scribner's remark that the enemy was "behind their ever-attending breastworks" is hard to reconcile since neither Kelly's nor Lowery's troops had time to construct them.

8. George H. Puntenny, *History of the Thirty-Seventh Regiment of Indiana Infantry Volunteers* (Rushville, IN: Jacksonian Book & Job Department, 1896), 89-92; J. T. Gibson, *History of the Seventy-Eighth Pennsylvania Volunteer Infantry* (Pittsburgh, PA: Press of the Pittsburgh Print Co., 1905), 147-50.

9. Puntenny, *History of the Thirty-Seventh Regiment of Indiana Infantry Volunteers*, 82-92.

10. Gibson, *History of the Seventy-Eighth Pennsylvania*, 147-50; Puntenny, *History of the Thirty-Seventh Regiment of Indiana Infantry Volunteers,* 89-92.

11. 38 OR 3:725; 38 OR 1:596; William R. Scaife, *The Campaign for Atlanta* (Cartersville, GA: Scaife Publications, 1993), 51; Puntenny, *History of the Thirty-Seventh Regiment of Indiana Infantry Volunteers*, 89-92.

12. 38 OR 1:378, 424; Stan C. Harley, "Govan's Confederate Brigade at Pickett's Mill," *Confederate Veteran* 12 (February 1904); George W. Tabor, "About the Battle of New Hope Church," *Confederate Veteran* 9 (September 1901).

13. Quoted in Castel, *Decision in the West*, 240.

14. 38 OR 1:195, 379, 866.

15. Howard, "The Struggle for Atlanta," 308.

Chapter Eleven

1. Symonds, *Stonewall of the West*, 213; Foster, *One of Cleburne's Command*, 85.

2. 38 OR 3:725; Symonds, *Stonewall of the West*, 253.

3. 38 OR 1:595; Foster, *One of Cleburne's Command*, 85; O. A. Buslett, *The Fifteenth Wisconsin*, trans. Barbara G. Scott (Ripon, WI: B.G. Scott, 1999), 552.

4. Foster, *One of Cleburne's Command*, 85-86.

5. Ibid., 85; Buslett, *The Fifteenth Wisconsin*, 546.

6. 38 OR 3:726; Foster, *One of Cleburne's Command*, 86.

7. Ibid.

8. Gay, *Life in Dixie During the War*, 89-90.

9. 38 OR 3:616; John Bell Hood, *Advance and Retreat: The Autobiography of General J. B. Hood* (1880; reprint, New York: Konecky & Konecky, n.d), 120-21. There is a disagreement among historians as to the date of Hood's planned attack. The accounts of Hood, Johnston, and Wheeler date the event as the night of May 28 through the morning of the twenty-ninth, which is apparently in error. These postwar accounts are refuted by most historians including Castel and McMurry, who have determined that Hood's sortie actually occurred on the night of May 27 and the early morning of the twenty-eighth. In any case, the argument loses significance after considering the fact that the attack was never made.

10. Symonds, *Joseph E. Johnston*, 298-99, 310, 324-25; Connelly, *Autumn of Glory*, 321-22, 417, 432; Richard M. McMurry, *John Bell Hood and the War for Southern Independence* (Lexington: University Press of Kentucky, 1982), 118.

11. Connelly, *Autumn of Glory*, 432; Hood, *Advance and Retreat*, 131-32, 162, 191-92; Hood's Texans quoted in John Bowers, *Chickamauga and Chattanooga*, 130; "Charge into the cauldron . . ." quoted in John Bowers, *Chickamauga and Chattanooga*, 82.

12. Williams, *This War So Horrible*, 84-85; Hood, *Advance and Retreat*, 121-22.

13. Ibid.; Joseph E. Johnston, "Opposing Sherman's Advance to Atlanta," 270; Symonds, *Joseph E. Johnston*, 299; Connelly, *Autumn of Glory*, 356. Earlier in the campaign, Hood had advised against an attack at Adairsville, aborted the planned attack at Cassville, and then urged Johnston to retreat past the Etowah River.

14. Williams, *This War So Horrible*, 85.

Chapter Twelve

1. For several days after the battle, soldiers from the Thirty-seventh Indiana and Seventy-eighth Pennsylvania camped beside the burned-down mill. During this time, they "let the water out of the dam and caught a few fish and turtles," according to Sergeant Puntenny. Puntenny, *History of the Thirty-Seventh Regiment of Indiana Infantry Volunteers*, 89-92.

2. Gay, *Life in Dixie During the War*, 91; Oliphant, *Only a Private*, 63; Columbus Sykes to his wife, May 29, 1864, Letters and Documents Collection, Kennesaw Mountain National Battlefield Park Library, Kennesaw, Georgia.

3. Ridley, *Battles and Sketches*, 305.

4. Oliphant, *Only a Private*, 64; Castel, *Decision in the West*, 241. Dr. Philip Secrist, who has spent many years exploring the terrain of the battlefield and documenting trench locations and other physical features, estimates that more than seven hundred Federals were buried in the mass graves on May 28, 1864, near the position of Granbury's lines (see Secrist, *Sherman's 1864 Trail of Battle to Atlanta*, 81).

5. Foster, *One of Cleburne's Command*, 88.

6. 38 OR 3:725; Scaife, *The Campaign for Atlanta*, 52; *Augusta Chronicle & Sentinel*, 29 May 1864.

7. 38 OR 4:331; In *Memoirs of General W. T. Sherman,* Sherman never makes mention of the battle at Pickett's Mill, an omission that apparently irritated some of the Southern participants including Johnston, who criticizes his silence on the Confederate victory in postwar writings (see Johnston, "Opposing Sherman's Advance to Atlanta," 270).

8. 52 OR 1:697; Castel, *Decision in the West*, 242.

9. 38 OR 4:331, 339; Sherman, "The Grand Strategy of the Last Year of the War," in *Battles and Leaders of the Civil War,* ed. Robert U. Johnson and Clarence C. Buel, vol. 4 (1887; reprint, Edison, NJ: Castle, n.d.), 252.

10. McMurry, *Atlanta 1864*, 94-96 (Johnston quoted, 95); McMurry, *John Bell Hood and the War for Southern Independence*, 114.

11. 38 OR 4:745.

12. Castel, *Decision in the West*, 243-44, 247; William B. Bate, report on operations in Atlanta Campaign, Letters and Documents Collection, Kennesaw Mountain National Battlefield Park Library, Kennesaw, Georgia, 4.

13. Cozzens, *This Terrible Sound*, 241-42; "protect that leg," quoted in Cozzens, 242. Warner, *Generals in Gray*, 19.

14. Bate, report on Atlanta Campaign, 4-6.

15. For background and character of Forrest, see Robert Selph Henry, *"First with the Most" Forrest* (1944; reprint, Westport, CT: Greenwood Press Publishers, 1974), 13-21 ("That devil" quoted, 16); Forrest's comment on Armstrong's brigade quoted in Clement Evans, ed., *Confederate Military History*, vol. 10 (Wilmington, NC: Bradford Publishing Co., 1987), 291.

16. Frank A. Montgomery, *Reminiscences of a Mississippian in Peace and War* (Cincinnati: Robert Clarke Co., 1901), 170-73.

Chapter Thirteen

1. Watkins, *Company Aytch*, 138-39. Watkins, writing years later, has mistakenly identified Frank Armstrong as Gen. John C. Breckenridge. Perhaps his memory failed him or, from a distance, he may have believed it was Breckenridge, which mistake would be understandable. Both commanders were fine figures, tall and dark with drooping moustaches. In any case, Breckenridge was not present at the battle of Dallas, having been dismissed by Bragg after the debacle at Missionary Ridge (see Connelly, *Autumn of Glory*, 277).

2. Wills, *Army Life of an Illinois Soldier*, 250-51.

3. 38 OR 3:95, 131, 279; Albert Castel, *Tom Taylor's Civil War* (Lawrence, KS: University Press of Kansas, 2000), 123.

4. 38 OR 3:95; Watkins, *Company Aytch*, 138-39.

5. 38 OR 3:95-96, 131; Wills, *Army Life of an Illinois Soldier*, 250-51.

6. 38 OR 3:95-96; Scaife, *The Campaign for Atlanta*, 54. For an account of the formation of Wilder's "Lightning Brigade" and the unusual manner by which they came to be armed with the Spencer repeating rifles, see Cozzens, *This Terrible Sound*, 14-15.

7. Montgomery, *Reminiscences of a Mississippian*, 170-73.

8. Bate, report on Atlanta Campaign, 6.

9. Watkins, *Company Aytch*, 138-39.

10. Bate, report on Atlanta Campaign, 6.

11. William C. Davis, *The Orphan Brigade: The Kentucky Confederates Who Couldn't Go Home* (Baton Rouge: Louisiana State University Press, 1980).

12. Ibid., 222; Bate, report on Atlanta Campaign, 6.

13. John S. Jackman, *Diary of a Confederate Soldier: John S. Jackman of the Orphan Brigade*, ed. William C. Davis (Columbia: University of South Carolina Press, 1997), 132; Weller quoted in Davis, *The Orphan Brigade*, 222.

14. Kentuckians quoted in Davis, *The Orphan Brigade*, 222.

15. John K. Duke, *History of the Fifty-Third Regiment Ohio Volunteer Infantry During the War of the Rebellion, 1861-1865* (Portsmouth, OH: The Blade Printing Company, 1900), 137-40.

16. Davis, *The Orphan Brigade*, 223; Castel, *Decision in the West*, 246-47.

17. 38 OR 3:96; Jackman, *Diary of a Confederate Soldier*, 132; Castel, *Decision in the West*, 246.

18. Jackman, *Diary of a Confederate Soldier*, 133; Bate, report on Atlanta Campaign, 6-7.

19. Wills, *Army Life of an Illinois Soldier*, 250-51.

Chapter Fourteen

1. 38 OR 4:339-40.

2. Bull, *Soldiering*, 119.

3. Wills, *Army Life of an Illinois Soldier*, 248-54; Confederate private quoted in Losson, *Tennessee's Forgotten Warriors*, 150; *Mobile Daily Advertiser and Register*, 7 June 1864.

4. Norrell Diary, May 30, 1864; W. T. Sherman to John Sherman, June 9, 1864, Library of Congress.

5. 38 OR 3:849; Wills, *Army Life of an Illinois Soldier*, 248-54; Castel, *Decision in the West*, 248-49.

6. Castel, *Decision in the West*, 250; 38 OR 3:706-7, 988; Jackman, *Diary of a Confederate Soldier*, 134; Foster, *One of Cleburn's Command*, 90.

7. Crowson and Brogden, *Bloody Banners*, 70-71.

8. 38 OR 3:988; Wills, *Army Life of an Illinois Soldier*, 248-54.

9. Clemson, "Surprised the Johnnies."

10. Bull, *Soldiering*, 112-19.

11. Nugent, *My Dear Nellie*, 185.

12. Joel D. Murphree, "Autobiography and Civil War Letters of Joel Dyer Murphree of Troy, Alabama 1864-1865," *Alabama Historic Quarterly* 19, no. 1 (Spring 1957); Samuel Merrill, "Letters from a Civil War Officer," *Mississippi Valley Historical Review* 14, no. 4 (March 1928).

13. Wills, *Army Life of an Illinois Soldier*, 248-54; Nugent, *My Dear Nellie*, 185.

14. 38 OR 3:989; 38 OR 4:387.

15. 38 OR 4:357; Sherman, *Memoirs*, 514-15.

16. 38 OR 4:366-67.

17. 38 OR 4:352, 357, 367.

18. Wills, *Army Life of an Illinois Soldier*, 248-54; Hale, *The Third Texas Cavalry*, 222; Castel, *Decision in the West*, 260.

19. 38 OR 3:990.

20. 38 OR 3:749, 753, 755.

21. 38 OR 3:987-89; Hood, *Advance and Retreat*, 124. Hood's account, written years after the war during the acrimony between he and Johnston, is self-serving at best. His contention that Johnston had proposed the army retreat all the way to Macon, Georgia, is unlikely and in all probability a lie. At the same time, there is little doubt that his corps commanders were depressed over another retreat.

22. Foster, *One of Cleburne's Command*, 91.

Bibliography

Manuscripts and Collections

Bate, William B. Report on Operations in Atlanta Campaign. Letters and Documents Collection, Kennesaw Mountain National Battlefield Park Library, Kennesaw, Georgia

Norrell, Willam O. Diary. Kennesaw Mountain National Battlefield Park Library, Kennesaw, Georgia.

Pickett Family. "History of the Pickett Ancestors." Pickett's Mill Battlefield State Park Library, Dallas, Georgia.

Sherman, William Tecumseh. Papers. Library of Congress, Washington, D.C.

————. Papers. University of Notre Dame, South Bend, Indiana.

Sykes, Columbus. Letters to wife. Kennesaw Mountain National Battlefield Park Library, Kennesaw, Georgia.

Newspapers

Augusta Chronicle & Sentinel
Kennesaw Gazette
Memphis (Atlanta) Daily Appeal
Mobile Daily Advertiser and Register

Published Primary Sources

Bierce, Ambrose. "The Crime at Pickett's Mill." In *The Collected Works of Ambrose Bierce*. New York: Gordian Press, 1966.

Bull, Rice C. *Soldiering: The Civil War Diary of Rice C. Bull.* Edited by K. Jack Bauer. San Rafael, CA: Presidio Press, 1978.

Buslett, O. A. *The Fifteenth Wisconsin*. Translated by Barbara G. Scott. Ripcon, WI: B.G. Scott, 1999.

Crowson, Noel, and John V. Brogden, comps. *Bloody Banners and Barefoot Boys: A History of the 27th Regiment Alabama Infantry, CSA: The Civil War Memories and Diary Entries of J. P. Cannon M.D.* Shippensburg, PA: Burd Street Press, 1997; White Mane Publishing Company, Inc.

Chesnut, Mary. *Mary Chesnut's Civil War*. Edited by C. Van Woodward. New Haven: Yale University Press, 1981.

Clemson, John W. "Surprised the Johnnies." *National Tribune,* 30 September 1897.

Cope, Alexis. *The Fifteenth Ohio Volunteers and Its Campaigns, War of 1861-65.* Columbus, OH: Press of the Edward T. Miller Co., 1916

Duke, John K. *History of the Fifty-Third Regiment Ohio Volunteer Infantry During the War of the Rebellion, 1861-1865.* Portsmouth, OH: The Blade Printing Co., 1900.

Dunkleman, Mark H., and Michael J. Winey, eds. *The Hardtack Regiment: An Illustrated History of the 154th Regiment, New York State Infantry Volunteers.* Rutherford, NJ: Fairleigh Dickinson University Press, 1981.

Foster, Samuel T. *One of Cleburne's Command: The Civil War Reminiscences and Diary of Capt. Samuel T. Foster, Granbury's Texas Brigade, CSA.* Edited by Norman D. Brown. Austin: University of Texas Press, 1980.

Gay, Mary A. H. *Life in Dixie During the War.* Edited by J. H. Segars. 1892. Reprint, Macon, GA: Mercer University Press, 2001.

Gibson, J. T., ed. *History of the Seventy-Eighth Pennsylvania Volunteer Infantry.* Pittsburgh, PA: Press of the Pittsburgh Print Co., 1905.

Harley, Stan C. "Govan's Confederate Brigade at Pickett's Mill." *Confederate Veteran* 12, no. 2 (February 1904).

Hood, John Bell. *Advance and Retreat: The Autobiography of General J. B. Hood.* 1880. Reprint, New York: Konecky & Konecky, n.d.

Horrall, Spillard F. *History of the Forty-Second Indiana Volunteer Infantry.* Chicago: Donohue and Henneberry, 1892.

Howard, Oliver O. *Autobiography of Oliver Otis Howard.* 2 vols. New York: Baker & Taylor Co., 1907.

———. "The Struggle for Atlanta." In *Battles and Leaders of the Civil War,* edited by Robert U. Johnson and Clarence C. Buel. Vol. 4. 1887. Reprint, Edison, NJ: Castle, n.d.

Howe, Robert. "Dead at New Hope Church." *Confederate Veteran* 5, no. 10 (October 1897).

Johnston, Joseph E. "Opposing Sherman's Advance to Atlanta." In *Battles and Leaders of the Civil War,* edited by Robert U. Johnson and Clarence C. Buel. Vol. 4. 1887. Reprint, Edison, NJ: Castle, n.d.

Liddell, St. John Richardson. *Liddell's Record.* Edited by Nathaniel Cheairs Hughes, Jr. Baton Rouge: Louisiana State University Press, 1985.

Lowery, Mark P. "General Mark P. Lowery, an Autobiography." *Kennesaw Gazette,* 15 November 1888.

McDermott, Gregory C. "A Fierce Hour at New Hope Church." *National Tribune,* 28 October 1897.

Merrill, Samuel. "Letters from a Civil War Officer." Edited by A. T. Votwiler. *Mississippi Valley Historical Review* 14, no. 4 (March 1928).

———. *The Seventieth Indiana Volunteer Infantry in the War of the Rebellion.* Indianapolis: The Bowen-Merrill Co., 1900.

Montgomery, Frank A. *Reminiscences of a Mississippian in Peace and War.* Cincinnati: Robert Clarke Co., 1901.

Murphree, Joel D. "Autobiography and Civil War Letters of Joel Dyer Murphree of Troy, Alabama 1864-1865." Edited by H. E. Sterkx. *Alabama Historical Quarterly* 19, no. 1 (Spring 1957): 178-79.

Nugent, William L. *My Dear Nellie: The Civil War Letters of William L. Nugent to Eleanor Smith Nugent.* Edited by William M. Cash and Lucy Somerville Howorth. Jackson, MS: University Press of Mississippi, 1977.

Oliphant, William J. *Only a Private: A Texan Remembers the Civil War, the Memoirs of William J. Oliphant.* Edited by James M. McCaffrey. Houston: Halcyon Press, 2004.

Perry, Henry Fales. *History of the Thirty-Eighth Regiment Indiana Volunteer Infantry*. Palo Alto: F.A. Stewart, 1906.

Puntenney, George H. *History of the Thirty-Seventh Regiment of Indiana Infantry Volunteers*. Rushville, IN: Jacksonian Book & Job Department, 1896.

Ridley, Bromfield L. *Battles and Sketches of the Army of Tennessee*. 1906. Reprint, Dayton, OH: Morningside Bookshop, 1995.

Sherman, William T. "The Grand Strategy of the Last Year of the War." In *Battles and Leaders of the Civil War*. Edited by Robert U. Johnson and Clarence C. Buel. Vol. 4. 1887. Reprint, Edison, NJ: Castle, n.d.

———. *Memoirs of General W. T. Sherman*. New York: Literary Classics of the United States, Inc., 1990.

Simpson, Brooks D., and Jean V. Berlin, eds. *Sherman's Civil War: Selected Correspondence of William T. Sherman, 1860-1865*. Chapel Hill: University of North Carolina Press, 1999.

Strayer, Larry M., and Richard A. Baumgartner, eds. *Echoes of Battle: The Atlanta Campaign*. Huntington, WV: Blue Acorn Press, 2004.

Tabor, George W. "About the Battle of New Hope Church." *Confederate Veteran* 9 (September 1901).

Taylor, F. Jay, ed. *Reluctant Rebel: The Secret Diary of Robert Patrick 1861-1865*. Baton Rouge: Louisiana State University Press, 1959.

Tuttle, John W. *The Union, the Civil War and John W. Tuttle: A Kentucky Captain's Account*. Edited by Hambleton Tapp and James C. Klotter. Frankfort, KY: Kentucky Historical Society, 1980.

U.S. War Department. *The War of the Rebellion: A Compilation of the Official Records of the Union and Confederate Armies*. 128 vols. Washington, D.C.: Government Printing Office, 1880-1901.

Watkins, Sam. *Company Aytch: Or, a Sideshow of the Big Show*. 1882. Reprint, New York: Collier Books, 1962.

Williams, Alpheus S. *From the Cannon's Mouth: The Civil War Letters of General Alpheus S. Williams*. Edited by Milo M. Quaife. Lincoln: University of Nebraska Press, 1995.

Williams, Hiram Smith. *This War So Horrible: The Civil War Diary of Hiram Smith Williams*. Edited by Lewis N. Wynne and Robert A. Taylor. Tuscaloosa: University of Alabama Press, 1993.

Wills, Charles W. *Army Life of an Illinois Soldier*. Washington, D.C.: Globe Printing Co., 1906.

Yeary, Mamie, comp. *Reminiscences of the Boys in Gray, 1861-1865*. Dayton, OH: Morningside House, 1986.

Secondary Sources

Bohmfalk, Frederick H. "Cleburne's Victory at the Pickett Settlement." In *A Meteor Shining Brightly: Essays on Maj. Gen. Patrick R. Cleburne*, edited by Mauriel Phillips Joslyn. Milledgeville, GA: Terrell House Publishing, 1998.

Bowers, John. *Chickamauga and Chattanooga: The Battles That Doomed the Confederacy*. New York: Avon Books, 1994.

Castel, Albert. *Decision in the West: The Atlanta Campaign of 1864*. Lawrence, KS: University Press of Kansas, 1992.

———. *Tom Taylor's Civil War*. Lawrence, KS: University Press of Kansas, 2000.

Connelly, Thomas L. *Army of the Heartland: The Army of Tennessee 1861-1862*. Baton Rouge: Louisiana State University Press, 1967.

————. *Autumn of Glory: The Army of Tennessee 1862-1865.* Baton Rouge: Louisiana State University Press, 1971.

Cozzens, Peter. *The Shipwreck of Their Hopes: The Battles for Chattanooga.* Chicago: University of Illinois Press, 1994.

————. *This Terrible Sound: The Battle of Chickamauga.* Chicago: University of Illinois Press, 1992.

Daniel, Larry J. *Cannoneers in Gray: The Field Artillery of the Army of Tennessee, 1861-1865.* Tuscaloosa: University of Alabama Press, 1984.

————. *Soldiering in the Army of Tennessee: A Portrait of Life in a Confederate Army.* Chapel Hill: University of North Carolina Press, 1991.

Davis, William C. *The Orphan Brigade: The Kentucky Confederates Who Couldn't Go Home.* Baton Rouge: Louisiana State University Press, 1980.

Elliott, Sam Davis. *Soldier of Tennessee: General Alexander P. Stewart and the Civil War in the West.* Baton Rouge: Louisiana State University Press, 1999.

Evans, Clement. ed. *Confederate Military History Extended Edition.* 17 vols. Wilmington, NC: Bradford Publishing Co., 1987.

Evans, David. *Sherman's Horsemen: Union Cavalry Operations in the Atlanta Campaign.* Bloomington: Indiana University Press, 1996.

Glatthaar, Joseph T. *Partners in Command: The Relationships Between Leaders in the Civil War.* New York: The Free Press, 1994.

Hale, Douglas. *The Third Texas Cavalry in the Civil War.* Norman, OK: University of Oklahoma Press, 1993.

Hallock, Judith Lee. *Braxton Bragg and Confederate Defeat.* Vol. 2. Tuscaloosa: University of Alabama Press, 1991.

Henry, Robert Selph. *"First with the Most" Forrest.* 1944. Reprint, Westport, CT: Greenwood Press Publishers, 1974.

Horn, Stanley F. *The Army of Tennessee.* Norman, OK: University of Oklahoma Press, 1953.

Hughes, Nathaniel Cheairs, Jr. *General William J. Hardee: Old Reliable.* Baton Rouge: Louisiana State University Press, 1965.

Hull, Mark M. "Concerning the Emancipation of the Slaves." In *A Meteor Shining Brightly: Essays on Maj. Gen. Patrick R. Cleburne,* edited by Mauriel Phillips Joslyn. Milledgeville, GA: Terrell House Publishing, 1998.

Joslyn, Mauriel Phillips. "A Moral and Upright Man." In *A Meteor Shining Brightly: Essays on Maj. Gen. Patrick R. Cleburne,* edited by Mauriel Phillips Joslyn. Milledgeville, GA: Terrell House Publishing, 1998.

Losson, Christopher. *Tennessee's Forgotten Warriors: Frank Cheatham and His Confederate Division.* Knoxville: University of Tennessee Press, 1989.

McMurry, Richard M. *Atlanta 1864.* Lincoln: University of Nebraska Press, 2000.

————. *John Bell Hood and the War for Southern Independence.* Lexington: University Press of Kentucky, 1982.

McWhiney, Grady. *Braxton Bragg and Confederate Defeat.* Vol. 1. Tuscaloosa: University of Alabama Press, 1969.

O'Connor, Richard. *Ambrose Bierce: A Biography.* Boston: Little, Brown & Company, 1967.

Scaife, William R. *The Campaign for Atlanta.* Cartersville, GA: Scaife Publications, 1993.

Secrist, Philip L. "Scenes of Awful Carnage." *Civil War Times Illustrated* (June 1971).

————. *Sherman's 1864 Trail of Battle to Atlanta*. Macon, GA: Mercer University Press, 2006.

Sword, Wiley. *The Confederacy's Last Hurrah: Spring Hill, Franklin, and Nashville*. Lawrence, KS: University Press of Kansas, 1992.

Symonds, Craig L. *Joseph E. Johnston: A Civil War Biography*. New York: W. W. Norton & Company, 1992.

————. *Stonewall of the West: Patrick Cleburne and the Civil War*. Lawrence, KS: University Press of Kansas, 1997.

Warner, Ezra J. *Generals in Blue: Lives of the Union Commanders*. Baton Rouge: Louisiana State University Press, 1964 and 1992.

————. *Generals in Gray: Lives of the Confederate Commanders*. Baton Rouge: Louisiana State University Press, 1959.

Index